KNOWING
YOUR
RIGHTS

HAMLYN HELP YOURSELF GUIDE

KNOWING YOUR RIGHTS

VINCENT POWELL-SMITH
DAVID CLARKE   JOHN PARKINSON
RICHARD TOWNSHEND-SMITH
CHRISTINE WILLMORE

HAMLYN

CONTRIBUTORS

PART 1   The Law and Your Money
Vincent Powell-Smith

PART 2   The Law and Your Leisure
Gambling   David Clarke
Holidays   John Parkinson
Sports & Pastimes   Richard Townshend-Smith
Using the Countryside   Christine Willmore

Published 1989 by
The Hamlyn Publishing Group Limited,
a division of the Octopus Publishing Group,
Michelin House, 81 Fulham Road,
London SW3 6RB.

Copyright © The Hamlyn Publishing Group Limited, 1987, 1989
First published in *You and The Law, 1987*

ISBN 0 600 56645 5

Printed and bound by The Guernsey Press

Contents

Introduction

Every day every one of us is affected by the law in one way or another, and yet we are often understandably vague about the increasingly complex body of laws which govern our actions. This book is designed to help you become more aware of your rights and obligations in certain important aspects of the law as it affects the consumer. The first part, *The Law and Your Money,* explains all about such matters as making purchases or sales, hiring goods, buying and selling on credit, and debts and financial problems. The second part, *The Law and Your Leisure,* covers such varied topics as gambling, holidays, sports and pastimes, and using the countryside.

Knowing Your Rights provides a fund of useful and up-to-date information for the general reader.

Part 1 The Law and Your Money

Buying and Selling Goods

1. Introduction

Buying and selling involves making a contract, which is an agreement which the law will enforce. Writing is not in general a requirement for a contract in English law, though there are some exceptions to this rule. Verbal agreements are quite valid and enforceable, and all that is required is an offer and an acceptance and 'consideration'. Each party must confer a benefit on the other because gratuitous promises are not binding unless made under seal. In the practical context of buying and selling, consideration is always present since the seller agrees to deliver goods and the buyer agrees to pay the price.

An offer is one party's indication of the terms on which he is willing to contract, but the contract only comes into existence when the offer has been accepted. There is usually no problem about this when the parties are negotiating face to face, as in a shop. For example, I go into a newsagent to buy the morning paper. I make the offer by telling the assistant the paper I want. He accepts the offer by handing the newspaper over. But there are cases where what might appear to be an offer is not in fact so in law. So, in the well-known case of *British Pharmaceutical Society v Boots Cash Chemists Ltd* (1952), it was held that the display of goods on the shelves of a self-service store was not an offer, but rather what the law calls 'an invitation to treat'. The customer makes the offer at the cash desk, and the assistant is quite free to accept or reject the offer. Similarly, the display of goods in a shop window is not an offer in the legal sense (*Fisher v Bell* (1961) nor is a catalogue or price list. This was established in *Grainger & Son v Gough* (1896) where a wine-merchant canvassed orders by sending out a price list. It was argued that the circular amounted to an offer in law. The Court ruled that it was not; it was an attempt to induce offers. The Court said:

'The transmission of such a price list does not amount to an offer to supply an unlimited quantity of the wine described at the price named, so that as soon as an order is given there is a binding contract to supply that quantity. If it were so, the merchant might find himself involved in any number of contractual obligations to supply wine of a particular description which he would be quite unable to carry out, his stock of wine of that description being necessarily limited'.

The practical consequence of this rule is that a shop is not bound to sell goods at the marked price or at all. This protects the shopkeeper, for example, if the price tag is wrong or in fact the goods are already sold.

Today's consumer is well protected by the law, and there is a large and growing body of consumer legislation, which is discussed in this section. As regards buying and selling goods, the main protection is contained in the Sale of Goods Act 1979 which sets out certain terms which apply in every case and gives the consumer valuable protection should the goods prove to be defective. The law relating to liability for defective goods is very complex, and there are three heads of liability: (1) liability in contract, ie, under the contract between the parties and on the basis of the Sale of Goods Act 1979; (2) liability in negligence if the goods are manufactured negligently and cause injury; (3) criminal liability, where statutory protection will apply, eg, under the Consumer Protection Act 1987.

2. Contractual Liability

In large-scale commercial transactions the parties often expressly agree on the contract terms, and go into considerable detail. The terms so agreed are called *express terms*. Terms can also be *implied* and this is the case under the Sale of Goods Act 1979. Not everything said between the parties during negotiations necessarily becomes a term of the subsequent contract. Untrue factual statements made with a view to inducing one party to contract may amount to misrepresentations, which will in themselves give rise to liability, but such statements must be distinguished from the seller's age-old overcommendation of his wares, which the law regards as 'mere puffs' which nobody is expected to believe.

The modern judicial tendency is to impose liability if it is possible to do so, as is well illustrated by *Andrews v Hopkinson*(1956), where a second-hand car dealer's sales manager assured a commercial traveller, George Andrews, who knew little about cars, that 1934 Standard saloon car was 'a good little bus' and added 'I would stake my life on it. You will have no trouble with it.' Mr Andrews agreed to take the car on hire purchase terms from a finance company and acknowledged in a delivery note that he was satisfied as to the car's condition. The steering mechanism was grossly defective, and the defect could have been discovered by a competent mechanic. It was held that quite apart from the contract with the finance company there was a contract between Mr. Andrews and the dealer, under which the latter guaranteed the car.

Sections 13 to 15 of the Sale of Goods Act 1979 lay down certain terms which will be implied in every contract of sale and these cannot be excluded in consumer sales. These implied terms are as follows.

(i) Description
If the consumer orders goods by description, they must correspond to the description. Most sales of goods are sales by description since the sale may fall into that category even though the buyer has himself selected the goods from stock without anything being said, as in the case of self-service stores where the customer selects the goods from the shelves.

(ii) Merchantability and Fitness for Purpose
Section 14 of the Sale of Goods Act 1979 sets out two implied conditions which are in fact interrelated and which apply 'where the seller sells goods in the course of a business'. This in fact excludes few cases other than that of the private seller, since the Act does not say 'in the course of the business of selling goods'. The two conditions are that the goods must be of 'merchantable quality' and also that they must be reasonably fit for the purpose for which they are bought.

What is meant by 'merchantable quality'? Section 14(6) gives a rather generalised answer. It says that goods are of merchantable quality 'if they are as fit for the purpose or purposes for which goods of that kind are commonly bought as it is reasonable to expect having regard to any description applied to them, the price (if relevant) and all the other relevant circumstances'. Merchantability relates to the actual condition of the goods, and the condition is applied to both new and second-hand goods. In the case of a second-hand sale, the description and the price are very important factors in deciding whether the goods fulfil their function. A car that does not start is clearly not of merchantable quality, but what of a new car whose engine seizes up after 142 miles?

This was the very point in *Bernstein v Pampsons Motors (Golders Green) Ltd* (1986). Mr Bernstein claimed £8,027.90, the price of a new Nissan Laurel car, petrol and taxi fare, from the supplying garage Pampsons Motors Ltd. In December 1984 the garage supplied the car which was to break down after 142 miles. The engine seized up because a piece of sealing compound was loose inside it. Mr Bernstein rejected the car but Pampsons Motors Ltd refused to refund the price, offering instead to repair the vehicle. The garage denied any breach of contractual obligations.

Counsel for Mr Bernstein told the court: Mr Bernstein's reaction was entirely reasonable. He wanted no further part in this car. There is only one issue. Was the condition of the car such at the time of delivery that there was a breach of the implied terms of reasonable fitness for its purpose and merchantable quality?

The judge held that this was a breach of the Sale of Goods Act in that the car was not of merchantable quality but he considered that in driving the car for a period of three weeks and 142 miles Bernstein had accepted the vehicle. He was not therefore entitled to rescission of the contract and repayment of the purchase price. He was awarded damages to compensate him for the cost of getting home, the loss of a tank of petrol, a totally spoilt day and the inconvenience of being without the car while it was being repaired. The judge said that had there been evidence that the car's value had been reduced as a result of the seizure and its repair, Mr Bernstein would have been entitled to damages for that too.

Two issues are raised by this case:
(i) Merchantable Quality. The nature of the problem, a drop of sealant which had got into the lubrication system when the car was assembled, subsequently depriving the camshaft of the lubrication and causing the engine to seize, meant both a risk of knock-on damage by stress to other parts of the engine and a potential danger. These two factors, in particular, led the judge to conclude that the car had not been of merchantable quality. (Case law has generally provided little support for complaining car owners unless their cars, new or old, have been unsafe. This factor again occurs here – the sealant in the engine was a potential danger if the engine had seized up whilst the car was in the fast lane of a motorway.)

The judge made some additional general comments on merchantable quality. In the case of mass production vehicles buyers had to put up with teething troubles and have them rectified. The buyer of a new car is entitled to expect more than from a second-hand one. The relevant factors are: price, time taken for repair, and a defect which is difficult to find and rectify. Rescission is not ruled out because a person tries to get an unmerchantable car put right.

(ii) Acceptance. The judge held that Section 35 of the Sale of Goods Act effectively disentitled the plaintiff to rescission if, after the lapse of a reasonable time, he had retained the car without intimating to the defendant that he was rejecting it. He said that Section 35 did not refer to a reasonable time to discover a particular defect; it meant a reasonable time to inspect the goods and try them out generally. The length of time would vary for different goods. On this basis Mr Bernstein had had a reasonable time to try the car out generally: in three weeks he had made two or three short trips for this very purpose.

There are two exceptions to the duty to provide goods of merchantable quality: (a) it does not apply where the goods are unmerchantable because of defects which have been specifically drawn to the buyer's attention before the contract is made; (b) it does not apply where the buyer has actually examined the goods before purchase in respect of defects which the examination ought to have revealed. Even a cursory examination brings this exception into operation, and so the buyer may be better off not to examine the goods at all.

The implied condition of fitness for purpose is covered by section 14(3) which says that in certain circumstances goods must be reasonably fit for the purpose for which they are bought. In order to bring section 14(3) into operation the following conditions must be met:

(a) The buyer must make known to the seller the purpose for which the goods are required so as to make it plain that he is relying on the other's skill and judgment. In practice this requirement is easily met. Where an article has only one natural purpose, merely asking for it is sufficient to make known by implication the particular purpose for which it is required. In *Jackson v Watson* (1909), for example, the request was for 'tinned salmon', and this was held to be sufficient to establish that the customer required the goods for eating;

(b) The sale must be in the course of business;

(c) The obligation does not apply 'where the circumstances show that the buyer does not rely, or that it is unreasonable for him to rely, on the skill or judgment of the seller. The seller is under an absolute obligation to see that the goods sold are reasonably fit for their purpose. He does not have to be at fault. So in *Jackson v Watson* (above) it was irrelevant whether, as would usually be the case, the grocer had no means of knowing that the tinned salmon was unfit for eating.

(iii) Sales by Sample

Where there is a sale by sample – usually, but not necessarily in the case of bulk commodities – the following terms are implied by section 15 of the Sale of Goods Act 1979: (a) that the bulk will correspond with the sample in quality; (b) that the buyer will have a reasonable opportunity of comparing bulk with sample; (c) that the goods will be free from defects, rendering them unmerchantable, which would not be apparent on reasonable examination of the sample.

(iv) Exclusion of Liability

An important question is whether the seller can, by express contractual terms, cancel the customer's rights to protection. In the case of the consumer sales, the seller's obligations under sections 13 to 15 of the Sale of Goods Act 1979 cannot be excluded. Any exclusion clause is made totally ineffective by section 6(2) of the Unfair Contract Terms Act 1977. A consumer sale in this context is one if: (a) the customer does not make the contract in the course of business nor hold himself out as doing so; (b) the other party does make the contract in the course of business; and (c) the goods concerned are of a type ordinarily supplied for private use and consumption.

Because of the provisions of section 6(2) – which outlaws exclusion clauses in consumer sales – if a customer wants to retain the extensive protection given by the Sale of Goods Act 1979, he must make sure that he does not unwittingly take himself outside the Act's protection. Obviously, a private sale between two private individuals is not a consumer sale, but there are borderline cases which are not always obvious. To save money, an individual may obtain a 'trade card' to enable him to buy from a wholesale warehouse at trade rates. This is probably not a consumer transaction because in fact the customer is holding himself out as a retailer.

The rights conferred by the Sale of Goods Act 1979 are against the seller. They are rights which arise in contract and so the customer's remedy (if anything goes wrong) is against the seller. Some shopkeepers will try and fob off dissatisfied customers by suggesting that his recourse is against the manufacturer. The legal position is that if the goods do not work properly, it is the shopkeeper who is primarily liable, for they are responsible for the fitness and quality of the goods which they sell.

(v) Untrue Pre-sales Statements

Untrue statements made by a seller in the course of negotiations leading up to a contract may be treated as terms of the contract, but then if not they may amount to *misrepresentations* and themselves give rise to liability. The customer can sue the seller if he made false statements of fact about the goods which induced the customer to buy them.

Statements of opinion do not amount to misrepresentations. If, for example, the customer is buying a television set and the salesman says 'I think the colour on this TV is the better of the two' the customer has no redress, in contrast to the situation where a car salesman says: 'This model has twin carbs'.

A purchaser who has bought goods relying on a misrepresentation is entitled to damages unless the person who made the misrepresentation can prove that he had reasonable grounds to believe it was true.

(vi) Manufacturer's Guarantees

Most major manufacturers of consumer durables give a 'guarantee' of the goods. The following wording is typical:

> 'The above-mentioned equipment is guaranteed against material or workmanship defects for twelve months after the date of purchase. In case of need, free in-warranty service shall be rendered by any one of the authorised service operators listed in this guarantee card, in accordance with the warranty policy and procedure explained in the operating manual, provided that the equipment has not been abused, altered, operated contrary to instructions, or repaired by unauthorised repair shops.'

These 'guarantees' are usually honoured by the manufacturer in practice, but in the normal case the customer wishing to rely on them must comply with any conditions laid down. Often these conditions include liability to heavy packaging-charges and, in some cases, to paying for any labour involved. In many instances it will be better for the customer to rely on his

13

Sale of Goods Act rights against the seller of the equipment. If, for example, you buy a camera from a chain-store and a few days later it becomes defective, the best course will be to seek redress against the chain store and either get your money back or obtain a replacement.

Unless the goods which are the subject of the 'guarantee' have been bought directly from the manufacturer – by post, for example – (when there will be a contract of sale and the Sale of Goods Act will apply) the guarantee may be legally worthless and ineffective. If the goods are bought from a retailer, the contract is between the retailer and customer; there will be no contractual relationship with the manufacturer.

The legal position is not, however, entirely clear, and in those cases where (as is often the case) the customer is required to return the guarantee card to the manufacture, including a good deal of information about the customer's age group, occupation and so on, it may be that their terms of the guarantee are directly enforceable as between customer and manufacturer, though it would take litigation to establish the position!

Your rights at sales

The Sale of Goods Act 1979 applies to purchases at sale time just as it does to other consumer purchases. This means that the goods must (a) be of merchantable quality; (b) correspond with description; (c) be reasonably fit for their purpose. Many sale goods are sold as 'seconds' or 'slightly defective'. You must accept minor defects. If things go wrong the the goods, notify the shop immediately. Notices saying 'No refunds on sale goods' or 'No refunds without a receipt' are not binding on you. They are illegal and your rights cannot be taken away by them. You are not bound to accept a credit note or an exchange. If the goods are seriously defective, you have a right to your money back. You are not entitled to your money back if you simply changed your mind. Failing satisfaction with the shop, complain to the local authority Consumer Advice Department. If all else fails, you can go to Court. There is a special 'small claims' procedure in the County Court.

The position is different where a payment is made in respect of the 'guarantee', as is often the case with consumer durables such as washing machines, television sets, and so forth, when the customer is paying for the item to be either serviced on a regular basis or repaired on call.

3. Liability in Negligence – Direct Claims Against Manufacturers

The consumer's usual remedy in respect of defective goods is against the person who sold the goods to him. But, quite independently of this liability

– which is based upon contract – someone who is injured by defective goods may have a claim against the manufacturer or, indeed, against the wholesaler or other intermediaries, any of whom may have to answer if the goods are defective and cause damage. This liability does not depend upon a contractual relationship; it is an independent liability imposed by the law of tort, and in particular by that specific tort or legal wrong called negligence. The basic principle was stated by the House of Lords more than 50 years ago in these words:

> 'A manufacturer of products, which he sells in such a form as to show that he intends them to reach the ultimate consumer in the form in which they left him with no reasonable possibility of intermediate examination, and with the knowledge that the absence of reasonable care in the preparation or putting up of the products will result in an injury to the consumer's life or property, owes a duty to the consumer to take reasonable care'.
>
> [Lord Atkin in *Donoghue v Stevenson*(1932)]

Subsequent case law has extended the meaning of the word 'manufacturers'; it covers wholesalers, retailers, and a wide variety of other people. And the principle is not limited to sales of goods, but extends to those who supply goods by way of hire purchase, hire, and so on, as well as to those who repair goods. So, in *Stennett v Hancock* (1939), a lorry-repairer negligently replaced a wheel which flew off and struck a passer-by. The repairer was held liable for the pedestrian's injuries.

Donoghue v Stevenson (1932) is still the leading case, and its facts are unforgettable. Mrs Donoghue and a friend went to a café, and the friend purchase a bottle of ginger beer, manufactured by Stevenson. The ginger beer was in an opaque bottle and, in fact, contained the decomposed remains of a snail. Mrs Donoghue became very ill as a result of imbibing the contaminated ginger beer. She could not sue the retailer (the proprietor of the café) because it was the friend and not she who had bought the ginger beer, but instead sued the manufacturer. Her claim was successful, and her case became the foundation of the modern law.

In a negligence claim, it is for the consumer to show that the manufacturer etc was careless, but a court may easily infer that snails do not find their way into carefully bottled ginger beer. The need to prove negligence can be very important in relation to newly discovered products, such as pharmaceuticals. So a major problem for the victims of thalidomide was to show that the manufacturers and distributors ought to have known that it was dangerous to foetuses. It is virtually certain that legislation will be introduced to remove the need to prove negligence where defective products lead to personal injury. At the moment it seems that the manufacturer cannot be sued simply because the product is defective: it is necessary to show that the product has caused personal injury or damage to property.

There is a new law relating to negligence under the Consumer Protection Act, which is covered in the next section.

4. Statutory Protection

Despite the availability of legal aid and advice, going to law is both costly and uncertain, although there are many organisations which will help the consumer in particular situations: see below. Another line of approach where the goods are defective is through the medium of the criminal law; this will not result in any financial recompense as such to the consumer, but merely in the person in default being subjected to criminal penalties, such as a fine. There is now a broad spectrum of legislation protecting the consumer, the advantage being that its enforcement lies in the hand of central and local government officials.

(i) The Trade Descriptions Act 1968
This is the most important single consumer protection legislation, and about 30,000 prosecutions are brought under its provisions every year. Its enforcement lies in the hands of the Trading Standards Department of the local authority, to whom complaints may be made.

Section 1(1) of the 1968 Act says:

'Any person who, in the course of a trade or business: (a) applies a false trade description to any goods; or (b) supplies or offers to supply any goods to which a false trade description is applied; shall, subject to the provisions of this Act, be guilty of an offence'.

The case law establishes that this provision is very wide in its scope. Many statements which would not give rise to civil liability in the law of contract have been held to be 'false trade descriptions' for the purposes of the Act, and in general liability under the Act does not depend on proof that the person applying the trade description knew it to be false. In some cases, however, the seller can disclaim liability for a false trade description, provided the disclaimer is 'as bold, precise and compelling as the trade description itself and [is] effectively brought to the notice of any person to whom the goods may be supplied' (*Norman v Bennett* (1974)) as, for example, by pasting a notice over the mileometer of a second-hand car stating that 'The accuracy of the recorded mileage is not guaranteed'. False or misleading indications as to the price of goods were prohibited by section 11 of the 1968 Act, (now covered by Part Three of the Consumer Protection Act, 1987), which creates three separate offences:
(a) *False comparisons with a recommended price.* It is unlawful for someone to offer to supply goods giving a false indication that their price is equal to or less than the price recommended by the manufacturer, though

16

there is a loophole where the manufacturer recommends a price so high that all retailers sell the goods well below that price;

(b) *False comparisons with the retailer's own price.* This is especially important in respect of goods bought in retailer's sales. It is an offence for a retailer to make false price comparisons with his own previous price unless in fact he has offered the goods at a higher price for a period not less than 28 days in the preceding six months. The protection is not so wide as appears because (a) in the case of multiple stores all that is required is to show that the goods were in fact offered at a higher price elsewhere and (b) the retailer can state that he has offered the goods at the higher price only

Consumers' Association
2 Marylebone Rd
London NW1   Tel. 01-486 5544

Consumers in the European Community
Group (CECG)
24 Tufton Street
London SW1 3RB   Tel. 01-222 2661

Consumer Credit Trade Association
159 Great Portland Street
London W1N 5FD   Tel. 01-636 7564

Consumer Credit Association of the United Kingdom (CCAUK)
Queens House
Queens Road
Chester CH1 3BQ   Tel. (0244) 312044

Institute of Consumer Advisers (ICA)
Flat 6, 24 Rye Lane
London SE15 5BS   Tel. 01-639 7079

National Federation of Consumer Groups (NFCG)
12 Mosley Street
Newcastle upon Tyne NE1 1DE   Tel. (091) 261 8259

Research Institute for Consumer Affairs (RICA)
2 Marylebone Rd
London NW1   Tel. 01-935 2460

for a short period. This is illustrated by *Westminster City Council v Ray Alan (Manshops) Ltd* (1982), where the accused put casual sweaters on sale at its Oxford Street, London W1, shop for 75p, with a tag saying 'Fantastic Reductions!'. It was held that the accused was entitled to establish as a defence that the 'fantastically reduced' sweaters had in fact been offered for sale at higher prices in its shops in Rotherham and Leeds!;

(c) *Indicating that the price is less than that actually being charged.* It is an offence to suggest that the customer is in fact being charged less than he actually is. So, for example, in *Sweeting v Northern Upholstery Ltd* (1982), Northern Upholstery advertised: 'Envoy suites in dralon at £699'. Only suites covered in beige dralon were in fact available at this price; if the customer wanted other colours he had to pay more. The advertisement was held to constitute an offence.

Not all price comparisons are caught by the provisions of section 11 of the Trade Descriptions Act 1968 nor is all misleading advertising caught by the Act. However, under the Price Marketing (Bargain Offers) Order 1969 the following comparisons are prohibited:(a) 'Worth £50, yours for £25'; (b) 'Save up to half price'; (c) 'At least £100 elsewhere, only £75'.

The 1968 Act does not only apply to trade descriptions about goods; section 14 also covers services, though in this case the defendant must have known that the statement which he was making was true or else have made it recklessly. The situation is illustrated by the case of *Wings Ltd v Ellis* (1984), where Wings' holiday brochure for 1981-82 winter season mistakenly indicated that certain hotel accommodation in Sri Lanka was air-conditioned, when it was not. In May 1981 Wings discovered the mistake and immediately took steps to correct the error by circularising travel agents. In January 1982 a customer booked a holiday with Wings through a travel agent relying on an uncorrected brochure, and neither Wings nor the travel agent informed him that the hotel was not air-conditioned. On his return home he complained both to Wings and to his local trading standards officer. The House of Lords held that Wings were properly convicted under section 14. A great many of the cases under section 14 have, in fact, involved holiday operators or airlines, and those who have been subjected to the common airline practice of overbooking can take comfort from the ruling in *British Airways Board v Taylor* (1976), where the airline issued a ticket to a passenger confirming his reservation for a named flight. The court very properly held that the statement that the seat was confirmed was a false statement even though, at the time the statement that the seat was confirmed was made, the flight was not then overbooked.

There are defences available to someone charged with an offence under the Trade Descriptions Act 1968. Section 24(1) provides that it is generally a defence to show: (a) that the commission of the offence was due to a mistake or reliance on information supplied to him by a third person, or to that person's act or default, or to an accident or some other cause beyond his control; and, (b) that he took all reasonable precautions and exercised all due care to avoid the commission of the offence by himself or his employees, etc.

(ii) The Consumer Protection Act 1987 (CPA)
Part One deals with Product Liability, Part Two with the general safety requirements and Part Three with misleading price indications.
Part One: Product liability under the Consumer Protection Act 1987 This Act

followed a European directive on product liability and introduced into UK law the concept of strict liability for defective products. It removes the need to prove negligence. Buyers of defective products have been able, and will continue to be able, to sue the seller under the law of contract. But under this Act, others injured by those products (relatives, visitors or employees) who have no contractual connection, are able to claim unlimited compensation on death, and personal injury or damage to property where that exceeds £275. It is necessary to prove that the product was defective and that it caused injury or loss. For claims under £275 consumers will have to rely on other remedies in contract or in tort.

A defective product is defined in the Act as meaning that the safety of the product was not such as persons generally are entitled to expect. A court will take into account all the relevant circumstances, including the purposes of the product, any instructions and warnings and what might reasonably be expected to be done with it. Manufacturers, importers or those who market goods under their own brand names can be sued. Retailers and wholesalers can also be sued if they fail to identify those who supplied them with the defective goods.

There are a number of defences, including:

(a) that they complied with a statutory or Community obligation, ie a minimum standard (s4(1)(a)).

(b) that the defendant did not supply the product (s4(1)(b)).

(c) that the supply was not in the course of a business (s4(1)(c)).

(d) that the defect did not exist at the time the product was supplied to the end user (s4(1)(d)).

(e) that the state of the art at the relevant time was such that the defect could not have been discovered (s4(1)(e)).

(f) that the defect was due to the design of the other product in which the component was fitted, or to instructions given by the manufacturer of that other product (s4(1)(f)).

(g) that the product was not of a type ordinarily intended for private use and was not intended to be used as such by the consumer (s5(2)).

Part Two: General Safety Requirements. *Section 10* introduces a wide-ranging legal duty to trade safely. Up until this Act only certain specific goods were covered by safety legislation. Now all in the distribution chain are liable, with criminal sanctions, to supply to consumers goods which meet an acceptable standard of safety.

Consumer goods fail to comply with the general safety requirement if they are not reasonably safe having regard to all the circumstances including: instructions and warnings given on the keeping or consumption of goods, how the goods are marketed (S10(2)(a)), any existing published safety standards (S10(2)(b)), whether there were means to make the goods safer (S10(2)(c). It is a defence under this section that the goods were secondhand (S10(4)(c)). Section 11 contains the powers to make safety regulations.

Safety regulations which were made under the Consumer Protection Act 1961 and the Consumer Safety Act 1978 (both Acts now repealed) are still in force and cover a variety of goods ranging from babies' dummies, pushchairs, toys, cooking utensils to bunkbeds. Regulations made under the CPA 1987 include such items as cosmetic products and furniture and furnishings.

Section 12 sets out the offences which can arise as a result of a breach of safety regulations or as a result of failure to give information required by regulations.

Section 13 gives the Secretary of State power to serve a 'prohibition notice' on a person prohibiting him/her from supplying etc. any specified goods and to serve a 'notice to warn' which requires a trader to publish information about goods which are considered unsafe. Notices issued include one prohibiting a Stockport-based company from exporting soap containing mercury compounds.

Section 14 enables enforcement authorities (trading standards departments etc.) to serve a 'suspension notice' on a person where there are reasonable grounds for suspecting that a safety provision has been contravened. The notice bans the person from supplying the specified goods unless consent is given. The suspension notice lasts for up to six months.

Section 16 empowers enforcement authorities in England, Wales and Northern Ireland to apply to a magistrate for a 'forfeiture order'. Where goods are ordered to be forfeited they are to be destroyed or disposed of as the court may direct. In two cases dangerous toy cookers have been forfeited and destroyed.

Section 17 concerns forfeiture in Scotland. A sheriff may make an order for forfeiture of any goods on application by a procurator-fiscal or where a person is convicted of an offence.

Part Three: Misleading price indications This part replaces section 11 of the Trade Descriptions Act 1968 and the Price Marking (Bargain Offers) Order 1979. It is backed up by a detailed code of practice. A person is guilty of an offence if in the course of any business of his, he gives (by any means whatever) to any consumers an indication which is misleading as to the price at which any goods, services, accommodation or facilities are available.

Section 26 gives the Secretary of State power to make regulations with regard to price indications.

Further Consumer Protection

Other consumer protection measures include the Fair Trading Act 1973 which set up the office of Director General of Fair Trading, who also has important responsibilities under the Consumer Credit Act 1974. Various important regulations have been made under the 1973 Act covering such things as business advertisements and mail order transactions.

5. Sales Between Private Individuals

So far as legal protection goes, you are generally better off buying from a commercial source, such as a retailer, since it is only in such cases that the full legal protections discussed in this section apply. Many sales, however, are made by private individuals, resulting from advertisements or from word of mouth. In private sales, only one of the basic Sale of Goods Act obligations will apply, namely that imposed by section 13, that 'the goods will correspond with description', but the private seller is under the same obligation as anyone else not to make false statements of fact ('misrepresentations')' Otherwise, the maxim of the law is expressed in the Latin tag *caveat emptor* – let the buyer beware.

6. Auction Sales

An auction sale is one where goods are sold to the highest bidder, and the very nature of an auction presupposes a conflict between the bidders and the vendors. The bidder wishes to purchase the goods as cheaply as possible, and the vendor wishes to obtain the highest price he can. Auction sales are, however, governed by the same basic principles of law as apply to other contracts of sale, although they are also subject to special rules. At an auction, it is the bidder who makes the offer by making his bid. The auctioneer's request for bids is merely an attempt to set the ball rolling. The auctioneer accepts the bid when the hammer falls and then the sale is complete. Neither party can then back out of the transaction, and the bidder is bound in law to pay for the goods.

Most auctions are governed by conditions of sale which are drawn up by the auctioneer – they will usually be printed in the catalogue and displayed in the auction room. At the outset of the sale the auctioneer will make it clear that all sales are subject to those conditions. Bidders are then bound by the conditions. Since these conditions are drawn up in the seller's interests, almost inevitably they will exclude liability for any defects in the goods bought. It is, therefore, essential to examine the goods carefully. It is quite usual for the conditions to exclude the Sale of Goods Act obligations of fitness for purpose, merchantable quality, and description as well as liability for 'misrepresentation' or false sales talk.

Section 6(3) of the Unfair Contract Terms Act 1977, allows this, subject to what it calls the test of 'reasonableness'. If there is a dispute as to whether or not the exclusion clause is reasonable, this is a matter for the court to decide 'having regard to the circumstances which were, or ought reasonably to have been, known to or in the contemplation of the parties at the time the contract was made' (section 11 of the 1977 Act) subject to guidelines set out in the Act.

The conditions of sale can also reserve for the seller or someone acting on his behalf the right to bid, thus pushing up the price. Well-drafted conditions of sale will also state whether or not the sale is 'subject to reserve', ie, a price below which the goods will not be sold. The auctioneer is not bound to disclose what the reserve price is, but if it is not reached, the goods will be withdrawn from the sale.

What happens where the sale is advertised as being 'without reserve'? Does this constitute a definite offer to sell to the highest bidder? The answer is probably yes.

What is clear is that an advertisement of an auction sale is not an offer in the legal sense. If, therefore, the sale is cancelled, disappointed would-be purchasers have no claim against the auctioneer. This was established in *Harris v Nickerson* (1873), where Nickerson advertised that some furniture would be sold by auction on a certain day. Harris attended the sale, but the lots in which he was interested were withdrawn. He sued Nickerson to recover for his loss of time and expenses involved in attending the abortive sale. His claim failed, the judge saying that it was 'an attempt to make a mere declaration of intention into a binding contract'.

The purchaser is not, however, entirely without protection. If, for example, he is induced to pay an inflated price at an auction by bids which, though apparently independent, were actually made on behalf of the vendor, he would not be bound by the sale unless, of course, the right to so bid had been reserved.

The auctioneer is the seller's agent. He works on a commission basis. The actual contract of sale is made between the buyer and the seller: the auctioneer is merely the intermediary. People selling goods at auction are also protected by the law. The auctioneer is liable for negligence in conducting the sale but, more importantly, auctions 'rings' are illegal. An auction ring is an agreement between intending bidders – usually dealers – whereby one or more of them do not bid, so as to damp down the price at which a lot is purchased or an arrangement under which the lots are to be divided amongst members of the ring either in agreed proportions or by a subsequent auction between them. Auction rings are prohibited by the Auctions (Bidding Agreements) Acts 1927-1969, but prosecutions are very rare because of the difficulties in establishing that a dealers' ring is in operation. The 1969 Act was introduced after a well-publicised affair in the late 1960s, in which a painting, which was bought for £2,700 at a country auction, was sold shortly afterwards to the National Gallery for £150,000. Suspicions that a dealers' ring was in operation were never proved, but the publicity led Parliament to strengthen the law.

Mock Auctions

A mock auction is one at which people are tricked into buying shoddy goods at grossly inflated prices. At one time this confidence trick was very common in London, at seaside resorts and fairgrounds. A variety of techniques were used, but usually the intended victims were lured by the promise of an auction at give-away prices. Attractive-looking goods were displayed, and these would then be auctioned. In each case, most of the money paid for the goods would then be refunded, so that the actual price paid was that stated at the outset. Once trapped, the bidders believed they were going to get bargains, and a number of expensive-looking items, which had not been on show, would be put up and sold to the bidders for many times their real value: the lots were often specially manufactured shoddy merchandise.

To remedy this situation the Mock Auctions Act 1961 was passed. This makes it a criminal offence – punishable by a fine of up to £1,000 and/or two years' imprisonment to promote or conduct, or to assist in the conduct of, a mock auction of lots including any of the following: plate, plated articles, linen, china, glass, books, pictures, prints, furniture, jewellery, household, personal or ornamental articles, musical instruments, scientific apparatus. A sales is a mock auction for this purpose if: (a) any lot is sold to a person at a lower price than his highest bid, or if part of the price is repaid or credited to him, unless this is to reimburse him for a defect discovered after he made his bid; or (b) the right to bid for any lot is restricted, or said to be restricted, to those who have bought or agreed to buy one or more articles; or (c) any articles are offered or given away as gifts. However, prosecutions brought under the Act are comparatively rare, and mock auctions still take place.

7. Buying Through Mail Order

6Buying goods by post is governed by the same principles of the law of contract as apply to any other sale. There are also some special rules. Advertisements or catalogues must include the supplier's name and business address.

The customer had the same legal protection as if he had bought the goods over the shop counter. The seller must supply goods which are fit for their intended use, of reasonable quality, and are as described. In fact, in buying goods by post the customer has to rely almost entirely on the description supplied in the catalogue or advertisement; if they are unsatisfactory and are not as described, he is entitled either to have his money back or to claim compensation, whichever is appropriate. If the goods are damaged in the post or in transit, this is the seller's responsibility, but the customer should take care to sign for any goods received from a carrier as 'unexamined' and then write to the seller immediately explaining the position.

Most reputable mail order concerns offer a 'money back guarantee' in any case, and many of the larger companies offer goods 'on approval'; the customer may return them if he is not satisfied, or even if he merely changes his mind. If goods are not sent 'on approval', then the customer can only claim the money back if there is something wrong with them.

Mail order customers are also protected by voluntary codes of practice which are in effect more stringent than legal controls. The Advertising Standards Authority (ASA), the Association of Mail Order Publishers (AMOP), and the Mail Order Traders Association all have codes of practice which protect the customer; most of the major newspaper and magazines take part in a scheme which guarantees the customer his money back if the advertiser's business becomes insolvent and the orders are not met. This scheme, however, only applies to 'display advertisements' and not to small advertisements in the classified columns. The main points to note are:

Mail order advertising protection
Advertisements in many magazines are governed by the British Code of Advertising Practice. Magazines participating in the scheme usually print a notice about it. Mail order advertisements which require payment in advance are covered by the Code. The advertiser must fulfil orders within 28 days unless he has stated a longer delivery period. The customer who returns the goods undamaged within seven days of receipt is entitled to his money back. If you return goods, make sure that you get proof of posting from the Post Office as you may need this receipt.

The Mail Order Protection Scheme usually applies. Where it does, and you pay for mail order goods in advance in response to an advertisement in the magazine, you may be able to get your money back from the publisher if the buyer becomes insolvent. You must write to the publisher not earlier than 28 days from the day you sent your order and not later than two months from that day if you have not received the goods or a refund. Claims made under the scheme will be honoured by the publisher if and when the advertiser is formerly declared bankrupt or insolvent. The scheme does not cover: (a) classified advertisements; (b) sales from catalogues, etc (only direct response sales are covered) (c) defective goods.

(a) Both the codes of practice adopted by The Advertising Standards Authority and The Association of Mail Order Publishers provide that 'cash with order' advertisements must state a waiting period of delivery – it is usually 28 days – and failure to meet this requirement should produce an automatic refund.

(b) The Newspaper Proprietors' Association Scheme has established a system for vetting prospective advertisers and, subject to the conditions of the scheme, will refund the money to the customer if the order is not fulfilled. It is wise to keep a copy of any advertisement or catalogue, and a copy of any correspondence.

24

8. Unsolicited Goods

Inertia selling is a well-known though dubious sales technique. Goods are sent which are not ordered in the hope that the recipient will pay for them. The same technique is applied to entries in trade directories: a business is sent a proposed entry in a 'trade directory' and then receives an invoice for payment. The Unsolicited Goods and Services Acts 1971 and 1975 deal with this racket, and make provision for the protection of those who receive unsolicited goods or services.

A customer is not obliged to pay for goods or services which he did not order and, as far as unsolicited goods are concerned, he has two options:

(a) He can keep the goods safe for a period of six months. They then belong to him and he can sell or dispose of them if he thinks fit. He can safely ignore any 'invoice' or request for payment, and need not return them at his own expense. But the sender is entitled to collect them during this six-month period. If they are not so collected the goods are treated as an unconditional gift;

(b) He can write to the sender stating that he did not order the goods and requiring them to be collected either from his address or another stated address. If the goods are not then collected within 30 days, they become his property.

During the six-month or 30-day periods the recipient cannot use the goods; he must store them safely, and not cause deliberate damage to them. The recipient is not, however, liable for accidental damage to the goods.

By going through the prescribed procedure the recipient can make the goods his property – but he must not unreasonably refuse to allow the sender or his representatives to collect them. It is a criminal offence – punishable with a fine of up to £200 – to send an invoice or demand for payment for any unsolicited goods, and if the sender threatens to take legal action, or tries to collect the 'debt' he faces a much heavier fine. In fact, the 'invoice' or demand seeking payment for unsolicited goods must state boldly in red: 'THIS IS NOT A DEMAND FOR PAYMENT – THERE IS NO OBLIGATION TO PAY'. This statement must appear at the top left-hand corner of the demand, which must also have boldly printed diagonally across the page 'THIS IS NOT A BILL'. There are similar controls over directory entries. The same legislation also makes it an offence to send any book, magazine, leaflet or advertising material for such items which describe or illustrate human sexual techniques if it is known or ought reasonably to be known that it is unsolicited.   Despite the legislation, this high-pressure sales technique is still common. Anyone who receives a threatening letter in respect of unsolicited goods or services should inform the police and/or the local Trading Standard Department.

9. Buying on the Doorstep

Many reputable firms employ doorstep salesmen, and the door-to-door salesman has the same legal obligations as any other seller of goods. The trouble with buying on the doorstep is that, if something goes wrong, it may be difficult to trace the salesman or his company. Doorstep purchasers should, therefore, ensure that they have proof of the salesman's identity, his address and the company's address. It may well be difficult to complain about faulty or unsatisfactory goods unless the firm is a reputable one.

Credit purchases made on the doorstep are subject to special rules. Briefly, when goods are bought on the doorstep on credit, such as hire-purchase, the salesman is usually obliged to give a copy of the contract to the customer who has a right to back out of the transaction within five days, the so-called 'cooling-off period'.

Under section 49(1) of the Consumer Credit Act 1974 to canvass certain types of credit on the doorstep – these include credit sales – is illegal but the prohibition does not apply if the salesman comes in response to the prospective customer's request which might, for example, be made through a newspaper advertisement. Broadly speaking, offering credit on the doorstep is illegal.

10. New Consumer Rights

From 1 July 1988, consumers acquired new legal rights when they agree to buy goods or service from a trader during an unsolicited visit to their home or place of work. The Consumer Protection (Cancellation of Contracts Concluded away from Business Premises) Regulations 1987 which came into force on that date provide for a seven day cooling-off period during which agreements covered by the regulations can be cancelled by the consumer without penalty. Traders are required to give their customers written notice of this right of cancellation and the name and address of a person against whom it can be exercised. These regulations implement a European Community Directive which provides a similar degree of protection for consumers throughout the Community.

Since 1985 the Consumer Credit Act has provided cancellation rights in respect of most credit and hire agreements signed away from trade premises. In addition many direct selling companies allow their customers a cooling-off period under codes of practice drawn up in consultation with the Director General of Fair Trading. These new regulations provide for the first time a statutory cooling-off period and cancellation rights for a wide range of cash sales made by traders who call on people at their home or place of work. They apply throughout the United Kingdom.

Repairs and Services

Contracts for repairs and services are basically governed by the Supply of Goods and Services Act 1982 and by the Unfair Contract Terms Act 1977, and these provisions give consumers valuable rights. Until the 1977 Act, many suppliers of goods and services traded on standard terms and conditions which limited the trader's liability or in some cases attempted to exempt him entirely if things went wrong.

Now, provided the contract is a 'consumer transaction', contract terms controlled by the 1977 Act are subject to the test of 'reasonableness'.

1. The Contractor's Obligations

Where a consumer employs a firm to carry out a repair or service, there is a contract between them. It is a contract for work and materials, ie a contract under which the contractor supplies both services and materials. The 1982 Act writes implied terms into contracts of this kind. The most important of them are as follows.

(a) *Where the contractor or supplier is acting in the course of a business, there is an implied term that he will carry out the work with reasonable care and skill.* The customer has the right to have the job done properly and to a reasonable standard. This is a very difficult test to apply in practice. The test is the average standard of the reasonably skilled member of the profession or trade in question. So, for example, in *Worlock v Saws* (1982), David Hicks was a carpenter by trade, but he had decided to branch out into general building work. Mrs Worlock wanted a small bungalow built and Mr Hicks agreed to build it. This was the first time he had undertaken responsibility for a new dwelling, though he had carried out some conversion work. He did the work badly in that he put in insufficient foundations. When sued by Mrs Worlock, the question arose as to the standard of care he ought to have shown. The court, while sympathetic to Mr Hicks, found him to be liable. His lack of experience did not help him. The judge said:

'The law is quite clear. He held himself out as a building contractor. He must therefore be judged as such because it was as a building contractor

27

that he was engaged . . . and . . . he was required to exercise generally over the work upon which he was engaged that standard of care which would be expected from a reasonably competent contractor'.

This ruling is of general application and all repair and service work must be done to a reasonable standard. If it is not, the contractor is in breach of this implied term.

(b) *Any materials used by the contractor will be fit for their purpose and of proper quality*. If a replacement part is fitted, it must be 'fit for its purpose', so if the customer takes a television set in for repair, he is entitled to expect that good quality replacement parts will be used.

(c) *Where no time is fixed for performance of the contract, there is an implied term that the supplier will carry out the job 'within a reasonable time'*. This is a question of fact. A complicated job will take much longer than a simple one, and what is a reasonable time in one case will not be so in another. It is always best to agree with the repairer how long the job should take.

(d) *The contractor has a duty to take reasonable care of the goods entrusted to him and to protect them from damage, fire and theft*. The contractor is liable if he is negligent but the law does permit the contractor to exempt himself from liability to a limited extent by means of an exemption clause printed in notices on the premises, receipts, tickets and the like. A typical garage exemption clause might read:

'We will not accept responsibility for any loss or damage sustained by the vehicle, its accessories or contents, however caused'.

An exemption clause of this type will in fact be valid to the extent that it is 'reasonable' under the Unfair Contract Terms Act 1977. Various factors are taken into account in deciding whether the clause is fair and reasonable and these include the customer's knowledge of the clause.

There is an important further control. Even if the clause would otherwise be valid, if its effect has been misrepresented to the customer by or on behalf of the contractor, it will not be enforceable. For example, in *Curtis v Chemical Cleaning and Dyeing Co Ltd* (1951), Mrs Curtis took a white satin wedding dress to the defendants for cleaning. The assistant asked her to sign a 'receipt' which contained a clause that the dress 'is accepted on condition that the company is not liable for any damage howsoever arising'. Before she signed, Mrs Curtis, asked why her signature was necessary. The assistant told her that the effect of the document was merely to exclude damage to beads or sequins. Mrs Curtis then signed the 'receipt' without actually reading it. The dress was badly stained. Mrs Curtis's claim for the cost of a new dress succeeded. The cleaners could not rely on the condition because, however innocently, they had misrepresented its effect to the customer.

2. Price of Repairs

It is always best to get an estimate or quotation before handing over goods for repair or servicing. Many firms have minimum charges, which can be quite exorbitant. In fact, where no price is agreed for the service, there is an implied term that the customer will pay a reasonable charge. This again is a question of fact, and the best guide is what other traders are charging, though the customer must expect to pay more for quick service. In most cases, a repairer can refuse to hand over the goods until he has been paid. In law, he has what is called 'a lien' over the goods.

3. Uncollected Goods

Sometimes customers fail to collect goods which they have left for repair or servicing. In such cases the repairman has a statutory right to sell them, after going through the correct procedure. If he knows how to contact the customer, the repairer must give the customer a written notice of intention to sell, which must be sent by registered letter or the recorded delivery service. The period between the notice and the proposed date of sale must give the customer 'a reasonable opportunity of taking delivery of the goods' and, when any payment is due, such as a repair charge, it must not be less than three months. If the repairer cannot notify the customer, because, for example, he does not have an address, he may be at risk in selling on the basis of not having taken 'reasonable steps' to trace him and so in such cases the repairer must be very careful.

In the straightforward case, if the customer fails to respond to the notice and collect the goods and pay the charge, the repairer can sell them, deduct the amount owing and the sale costs, and pay the balance over to the customer. The repairer must adopt the method of sale in the circumstances. This may mean selling expensive goods by auction and, indeed, if the goods are valuable, the wise repairer will apply to the Court for an order for sale, as this will then protect him.

These rules are set out in the Torts (Interference with Goods) Act 1977, which permits arrangements more favourable to the repairer to be made. Many repairers in fact write a term into their conditions or put a written notice up on the premises, to this effect. Under a specially agreed term, for example, the repairer may reserve the right to sell the goods after a shorter period and keep the profit.

Hiring Goods

Consumer hire contracts are often called 'rental agreements'. They are subject to control under the Consumer Credit Act 1974 which lays down very strict rules that must be complied with. They are growing in importance, and today almost anything can be hired: fancy dress, a morning suit for a society wedding or a car for a holiday, either on short or long term. Television sets and video recorders are often rented on a long-term basis, while such things as floor sanders, rotavators and so on are hired in the short term.

There is no legal significance in the terminology used by the owner: renting, leasing and hiring are synonymous in law. Unlike contracts for the sale of goods, under a hire contract ownership does not pass from one party to the other; the goods remain the owner's property, but the hirer has the use of them. Hire differs from hire-purchase in that the hirer never becomes the owner of the goods, however long the agreement may last. Under a hire-purchase contract the hirer has the opportunity of acquiring ownership of the goods and, indeed, that is the purpose of the transaction. Under a rental agreement there is simply a transfer of possession, subject to the owner's terms and conditions.

Section 15 of the 1974 Act contains its own definition of a 'consumer hire agreement'. It is an agreement: (a) other than a hire purchase agreement; (b) made with an individual hirer; (c) capable of lasting for more than three months; (d) where the hirer is not required to make payments exceeding £15,000

The Act also covers 'small agreements' under which the hirer is not required to make payments in excess of £50 and, effectively, all consumer hire agreements are covered. (The hire of telephone and metering equipment for British Telecom is, however, exempt.) There are strict rules about the way in which the hire agreement must be set out and what it must contain, and the main point for the consumer to watch is whether there is any minimum or fixed period of hiring. Hire concerns usually stipulate for a minimum period of hiring – which generally cannot be longer than eighteen months – and if the hirer wishes to terminate the agreement before that minimum period, he will have to pay an agreed sum for earlier determination. Most hire contracts in fact contain a minimum payment clause.

The situation is illustrated by *Robophone Facilities Ltd v Blank* (1966) where an accountant hired a telephone answering machine for a period of seven years, at a rental of just over £17 a quarter, the value of the machine being £350. Clause 11 of the agreement was a minimum payment provision, under which Mr Blank undertook to pay a sum equal to 50% of the total rental which would thereafter become payable. Immediately after signing the agreement Mr Blank changed his mind and purported to cancel the agreement. The Court ruled that he must pay £245 11s as compensation.

Subject to a few exceptions section 101 of the 1974 Act entitles the hirer to give written notice of termination after eighteen months from the date of the agreement. The period of notice must equal the intervals of payment, eg a week's notice if the rental is payable weekly, or three months, whichever is the less. Terminating the arrangement does not affect the hirer's liability to pay any overdue rent, and the section 101 provision does not cover agreements under which the annual payments exceed £900 (£17.31 a week or £75 a month).

A few hire contracts are for a fixed length of time; others run from week to week or month to month. In periodic agreements, the notice required to terminate will usually be laid down. If nothing is said, a notice equivalent to the period of hire is sufficient to bring the agreement to an end. Owners usually stipulate that the goods must be kept at a particular place, and can at any time require the hirer to give information about where the goods are. If the hirer fails to pay the rental due, the owner has the right to repossess the goods without a Court order, although he must give a default notice. The hirer does not have the same statutory protection against repossession as does the buyer under a hire-purchase agreement. However, where the owner has repossessed the goods, section 132 of the 1974 Act enables a Court, on the hirer's application, to order repayment to him of all or any part of his payments and cancel any sums owed by him. This power is rarely exercised and so far as cancellation of payments is concerned, probably refers to future payments and not existing liabilities.

1. Owner's Obligations

The supply of Goods and Services Act 1982 imposes certain liabilities on the owner of the goods under a contract of hire, which is defined so as to include all normal hire transactions. The owner's statutory obligations are:

(i) There is an implied condition that the owner has the right to hire out the goods for the period of the hire and that he will not interfere with the hirer's 'quiet enjoyment' throughout the hire period. It follows that the hirer can sue the owner if his possession of the goods is interfered with by a third person because, for example, the owner's legal title is defective. This is of importance where the hirer is dealing with an 'owner' who does not in fact own the goods because, eg, they are subject to a hire-purchase agreement.

(ii) There is an implied condition that the good will correspond to description.

(iii) Where the owner is supplying the goods in the course of a business, there are implied conditions that the goods will be of merchantable quality and reasonably fit for the particular purpose for which they are supplied. If the owner is in breach of these terms, the hirer can return the goods and treat the contract as at an end unless the owner can replace them or remedy the defect immediately.

In the case of consumer transactions, these terms cannot be excluded by a clause in the hire contract. In a non-consumer situation, they can be excluded to the extent that it is 'reasonable' to do so.

2. Hirer's Obligations

There are corresponding liabilities on the hirer. His obligations are:

(i) He must pay the agreed charge or rental at the times and in the manner specified in the agreement. Failure to pay will entitle the owner to serve a default notice, terminate the agreement and repossess the goods. The hirer is still bound to discharge any arrears and the owner may be entitled to claim damages. This can be important in the case of a fixed-term contract because then, in principle, the owner is entitled to recover the whole of the rental which would have been payable for the fixed period.

(ii) He must take reasonable care of the goods and observe any restrictions placed upon their use by the terms of the agreement. He is responsible if he carelessly damages the property. The hirer is not, however, an insurer and is not, therefore, liable if the goods are damaged by an accidental fire or if they are stolen. However, some hire contracts impose on him an obligation to insure the equipment for its fully value. There is usually an express term dealing with the hirer's responsibility for safekeeping, eg.

> 'THE HIRER is responsible for the safekeeping of the goods and for their use in a proper manner, and is strictly liable for any loss of or damage to the goods, from whatsoever cause arising, fair wear and tear excepted.'

A clause in this form makes the hirer strictly responsible and under it the hire would be responsible even if he was not negligent, thus altering the general rule.

The hirer is not under any obligation to repair the goods and, indeed most hire agreements provide that he 'shall not repair or attempt to repair the goods'. If he fails to observe the terms of a non-repair clause he is liable for any resulting damage.

(iii) He must return the goods at the end of the contract. Quite apart from his contractual liabilities, the hirer is liable under the law of tort. If he sells or disposes of the goods, he breaks the contract, and brings the hire arrangement to an end. Selling hired goods is also a criminal offence, quite apart from the fact that the owner can sue the hirer for the tort of conversion and claim damages. It also amounts to conversion if the hirer refuses to hand over the goods should the owner make a lawful demand for their return. The third party will not become the owner of the hired goods. The position is illustrated by *Hillesden Securities Ltd v Ryjack Ltd*(1983), where a car was leased for a period of three years and the hirer sold the car during this period. Hearing of the wrongful disposal, the owner demanded the car back. When its demand was not complied with, the owner sued for conversion. The car was in fact handed back after a few months, just before the Court case. The judge ordered the hirer to pay damages at the rate of £115 a week – the rental of the car – from the time of the 'sale' until the date when it was returned.

The Office of Fair Trading has produced a guidance note called 'Hire Agreements' which explains the rules about the form and content of hire agreements. Copies can be obtained from the local Trading Standards Officers or from the Consumer Credit Licensing Branch, Rooms 497/11, Government Buildings, Bromyard Avenue, Acton, London W3 7BB or from the Office of Fair Trading, Field House, Breams Buildings, London EC4.

Buying on Long-Term Credit

Apart from bank overdrafts and bank loans, there are three common forms
of credit under which the customer purchases the goods by instalments:
hire purchase, conditional sales and credit sales. There credit transactions
are all governed by the Consumer Credit Act 1974, which is one of the most
complex measures on the Statute Book. It was not until 19 May 1985 that
the last of its major provisions came into effect, and even now some of its
provisions are not in force. The Act largely regulates what are called
'consumer credit agreements' which are defined as a contract for credit: (a)
not exceeding £15,000; (b) made to an individual or group of individuals,
such as a partnership. The protection given by the 1974 Act does not
extend to limited companies. Most consumer credit transactions are caught
by the Act, few individual consumers buy anything worth more than
£15,000 on credit terms. The 1974 Act introduces its own classification of
credit-type purchases, and the statutory definition of credit is so elastic as
to catch transactions that have not yet been invented.

In law, hire purchase, credit sales and conditional sales are three distinct
forms of transaction:

(i) Hire purchase, strictly speaking, is not a sale. What the hire purchaser
is doing is agreeing to hire the goods for a period and pay the hire rent; at
the end of the period he has an option to buy the goods on payment of a
small additional sum. In *Helby v Matthews* (1895) the House of Lords ruled
that under a hire purchase contract, because the hirer is not legally bound
to exercise the option to purchase, the contract is not one of sale. The
result of this ruling is that during the currency of the transaction the hirer
does not own the goods and he cannot transfer ownership to someone else.
It is only on the exercise of the option to purchase that the ownership
passes to the customer.

(ii) A credit sale, in contrast, in its simplest form is a straightforward
contract for the sale of the goods. The buyer is allowed to defer payments
of the price or part of it. Usually there will be a schedule of payments. The
buyer will become the owner usually on delivery.

(iii) A conditional sale is different again. It is an agreement to sell. The
buyer gets the goods on payment of a deposit, and pays the unpaid balance

of the price in fixed instalments. Ownership does not pass to the buyer until he pays all the instalments. During the currency of the agreement, the buyer cannot transfer ownership.

In all cases, the liability for the condition and quality of the goods lies on the creditor – who may be the dealer or the finance company, depending on the technicalities of the transaction. The legal refinements do not generally concern the actual consumer because all these transactions are made on standard sets of documents which specify the type of transaction concerned.

Despite the protection afforded to consumers by the 1974 Act, it is necessary to be careful. Oral agreements for credit are allowed under the general law, which does not lay down special requirements unless the agreement is *regulated* by the 1974 Act, and if for some reason the agreement is not caught by the Act's provisions, the customer may be in a difficult position. Whatever the legal position, it is always dangerous to sign a form of agreement in blank and allow the dealer to fill in the details.

The dangers of doing so are graphically illustrated by *United Dominions Trust Ltd v West* (1975), where Eric Western wished to buy a second-hand Ford Corsair on display at the premises of Romanay Car Sales. As a result of discussions between Mr Western and Mr Romanay, Mr Western agreed to buy the car for £550, and paid a small deposit as he wished to buy on hire-purchase terms. He then signed what he took to be a standard hire purchase agreement, leaving the dealer to fill in the blanks. In fact, it was UDT's standard form of loan agreement, and the figures filled in were not those which had been agreed between Western and Romanay. The price of the car was put in as £730, and a larger deposit was mentioned. UDT accepted the transaction in good faith and sent Mr Western a copy of the agreement. He did nothing about it, but became dissatisfied with the car, which was later stolen. He failed to pay any instalments due under the agreement. The Court of Appeal held that he was bound by the terms of the document, and upheld the trial judge's order that Mr Western should pay £750, plus costs. Since most hire purchase and allied agreements are today caught by the 1974 Act, a similar case is not likely to arise, but the court's ruling emphasises how dangerous it is to sign a blank or partially-completed agreement.

Note. All consumer credit agreements within the 1974 Act are 'regulated agreements' unless exempted. There are no exemptions for hire purchase and conditional sale agreements.

1. Hire Purchase

A hire purchase agreement is defined (section 189(1) of the 1974 Act) as an agreement under which the purchaser takes the goods on hire initially, with

Buying stolen goods

The basic rule of the common law, affirmed by the Sale of Goods Act 1979, is that the sale of goods by someone who is not the true owner, or acting with his authority, cannot make the buyer the owner. He gets no legal title to the goods, even if he acted innocently and in good faith, and will be obliged to give the goods up to the true owner.

Buying stolen goods knowingly is a criminal offence – punishable with imprisonment – and the circumstances in which the goods were bought is always a factor which the police take into account in deciding whether or not to prosecute. It is not an offence to buy stolen goods unless the buyer knows or believes them to be stolen, and in practice stolen goods are often purchased innocently. Obviously, if a consumer buys stolen goods from a reputable source, and it turns out subsequently that the goods are stolen, and have to be returned to their true owner, the buyer will have a claim against the innocent seller, who is liable for breach of the implied term that he has the right to sell the goods. The innocent seller, in turn, would have a claim against the person from whom he bought, but eventually the chain comes to an end. This straightforward and simple rule is subject to a number of exceptions, but only two of them are of much practical importance:

(a) Where goods are bought in 'market overt' the buyer acquires a good title to them subject to certain conditions. A sale in 'market overt' is essentially a sale in a long-established market, on a market day, or any open sale in a shop in the City of London, for such things as are usually sold in the shop. The sale must be by and not to the shopkeeper, and must be of an item which is of a type usually sold in the shop. For example, a sale of jewellery in a grocery shop would not be a sale in market overt. The sale must also take place openly, that is in a saleroom to which the general public is admitted. Outside the City of London, the sale must be in a legally-constituted market, on a market day, and in accordance with the custom of the market. In both cases, the buyer will become the owner of the goods provided he buys them in good faith and does not know that the seller cannot transfer ownership.

(b) Of more practical importance, there are special statutory provisions relating to private purchases of motor vehicles which are in fact on hire-purchase or conditional sale terms. This exception is set out in part III of the Hire Purchase Act 1964. If a private purchaser buys a motor vehicle which is subject to a hire purchase or credit sale agreement, he acquires a good legal title to it if he bought in good faith and without knowledge of the hire purchase or credit sale agreement. The exception does not apply to dealers but, curiously, if a private purchaser buys such a motor vehicle from a dealer, he will become the owner of the car, even though the original sale was not effective to transfer the ownership to the dealer.

There is little justification for the market overt rule, which is a hangover from mediaeval days. Citizens' Advice Bureaux and the motoring organisations, such as the AA and RAC, can make searches of the records of Hire-Purchase Information Ltd (HPI). HPI was set up by the finance companies to prevent hire-purchase fraud, and member companies notify HPI of any motor-vehicle hire-purchase agreement which they enter into. HPI records the information and answers queries from member finance companies and motor dealers, and so on, but not from private individuals.

an option to become the owner at a later stage if he so desires. The form and content of hire purchase agreements is laid down by regulations, and it is important to realise that the financial limit of £15,000 (which brings the agreement within the statutory provisions) is not the price of the goods. It is the amount of the credit. The document must contain the following information and the first page must be headed prominently 'HIRE PURCHASE AGREEMENT REGULATED BY THE CONSUMER CREDIT ACT 1974':

(a) The names and postal addresses of each party;
(b) A description of the goods;
(c) Their cash price;
(d) The amount of the deposit, which is to include any part-exchange allowance;
(e) The amount of the credit, ie the difference between the cash price and the deposit;
(f) The total charge for credit, ie the sum of the last three items;
(g) The amount of each instalment;
(h) The Annual Percentage Rate (APR), ie, the actual rate of interest;
(i) Description of any security, eg, a guarantee by a third party;
(j) Details of any charges payable if the customer defaults.

The agreement must also set out, in a red box, a very clear warning: 'This Document contains the terms of a hire purchase agreement. Sign it only if you want to be legally bound by them.' The signature of the hirer is appended.

The goods will not become your property until you have made all the payments. You must not sell them before then.

Other information must be given in the document, and notably details of the hirer's rights on termination and the legal position about repossession. These statements must be printed boldly.

The customer will therefore always know if he is signing a hire-purchase agreement. Before he signs it he must be told the cash price of the goods, the rate of interest, and the total credit price; usually this is done by a label on smaller goods. It is not enough merely for it to be set out in the agreement.

Under a hire-purchase agreement, just as under an ordinary sale of goods, certain obligations are written in by statute. These are conditions that: (a) the owner or seller has the right to sell the goods; (b) the goods must be of 'merchantable quality' that is free from serious defects; (c) they must be reasonably fit for the purpose which they are required. Dealers or finance companies cannot exclude these implied obligations in a consumer contract of hire-purchase. The law protects the hire purchase customer in many ways, and in the majority of cases the customer can back out of the agreement within a short space of time. He is not necessarily legally committed because he has signed the agreement – he is moving towards a legal commitment. There are two cases to consider.

(i) Cancelling Before the Agreement Is Completed

At any time before the completion of the agreement, either party may withdraw from the transaction. This is the rule under the general law of contract but has special application in the field of hire purchase. Sections 62 and 63 of the 1974 Act stipulate that the customer must be given at least one copy, and often two copies, of the agreement. In the usual case, the customer will receive two copies. Suppose, for example, a customer has decided to buy a car on hire purchase terms. In the nature of things, the finance company will want to make inquiries about the customer's credit worthiness. So the dealer will fill out the form and the customer will sign and must be given a copy of the agreement. At that point it is not legally binding: it will not be binding until it is signed as accepted by the finance company, and this will often be several days later. So at any time before it is accepted by the finance company the customer can back out. If he decides to do so, he would be wise to send his cancellation by recorded post to both the finance company and the dealer, quoting the details of the transaction from the unexecuted agreement. Once the agreement has been accepted by the finance company, it is too late to back out – unless the agreement was made 'off trade premises': see below.

The customer is entitled to a second copy of the agreement, this time of the agreement as accepted by the finance company. This copy must be given to him within seven days following the making of the agreement, ie, when it was accepted by the finance company. The seven day period starts to run on the day following the making of the contract. This requirement is satisfied if the copy agreement is posted, even though it arrives after expiry of the seven day period.

(ii) Cancellable Agreements

For many years legislation has protected customers against the unfair pressure sometimes exerted by door-to-door salesmen and has given the customer the right to cancel the contract for a limited period – called 'the cooling-off period'. This applies whenever the customer signs the agreement away from the business premises of the dealer, the finance company, or the salesman. There is also a requirement that the salesman or negotiator should have made oral representations to the customer, but this requirement is invariably satisfied.

The agreement must then contain, immediately adjacent to the box for signature, a special and boldly printed notice: 'YOUR RIGHT TO CANCEL'. Once you have signed this agreement you will have for a short time a right to cancel it. Exact details of how and when you can do this will be sent to you by post by the creditor. However, the customer need not wait to hear from the finance company or other creditor, but he must exercise his right to cancel within the cooling-off period. The normal period runs from the time the customer signed the agreement to the end of the fifth day following the day on which he receives the second copy through the post. In effect, once he receives the document he has six days in which to cancel.

Cancellation must be by written notice posted or given by the customer. Finance companies often provide special forms, but no special wording is required. All the customers has to do is to write indicating his intention to withdraw from the agreement. Although the Act says that where a notice is posted it takes effect on posting, whether or not it is actually received, it is best to use recorded delivery post to avoid arguments. Cancellation destroys the agreement; it is treated as though it never existed, and the customer is entitled to receive back all the money he has paid, less a small fee.

(iii) Practical Problems
(A) Early settlement. Sometimes the customer will decide that it is in his interests to settle the agreement before the agreed date by offering to pay off the outstanding balance. Section 94 of the 1974 Act gives the customer a right to settle an agreement early by giving written notice to the finance company and paying off the outstanding balance, less a rebate for early settlement. There is a very complicated formula for calculating the rebate, and what the customer must do is to write to the finance company asking for a settlement figure. If the customer does then settle early, the agreement is at an end and the goods become the customer's property.

(B) Repossession of goods. Failure to make payments to the finance company as they fall due is a breach of the terms of the agreement. Since the goods are not the customer's property, the finance company is entitled to repossess them or claim them back. Many customers in fact fall into arrears through no fault of their own, and if this happens most of the finance companies will be reasonably sympathetic and will accept reduced payments or come to some compromise agreement. There are restriction on the finance company's right to repossess the goods in any case.

Once the customer has paid one third of the total credit price, the goods become 'protected goods' under section 90 of the 1974 Act. This means that the finance company cannot recover the goods without a Court order. The company must, in any event, serve a *default notice* in a special form and no action can be taken by the finance company until at least seven days after notice has been served.

There is, however, a loophole, even in the case of 'protected goods' because, having served a default notice, the finance company can recover possession if the customer consents. In some cases it will be to the customer's benefit to do this – but in others it is best to rely on the statutory protection because the finance company must then take Court proceedings. The judge will not necessarily allow the goods to be reclaimed. Indeed, if there is a reasonable period of time, it is likely that the court will make an order for the debt to be paid off by instalments.

Where the goods are not protected – because for example, less than a third of the credit price has been paid, no Court order is required. A default notice must still be served and in any case the finance company's representatives cannot come on to the customer's property to recover the goods without the customer's consent. Whatever the agreement may say, section 92 of the 1974 Act forbids the finance company from entering premises without a Court order. Indeed, any attempt to do so which is calculated to cause distress, alarm or humiliation to the customer or his family may well constitute a criminal offence.

2. Credit Sale Agreements

A credit sale agreement differs from hire purchase in that under it the customer becomes the owner of the goods immediately. He can, therefore, sell the goods while the agreement is running, though most credit sale agreements contain a clause requiring the immediate repayment of any balance due if the goods are sold. Credit sale payments are made on the basis of five or more instalments and interest rates are similar to those under hire purchase agreements.

Where the goods turn out to be unsatisfactory, the customer's legal rights are the same as in an ordinary sale of goods. The consumer cannot lose his legal protection by contrary term in the credit sale agreement.

The main difference between a credit sale agreement and a hire purchase agreement is that the seller cannot repossess the goods after the agreement has been made, even if the customer defaults on the instalment payments. The seller's only right is to sue for what is owed. Credit sale agreements are still subject to the requirements of the Consumer Credit Act 1974. The customer is entitled to be informed of the cash price of the goods, the total credit price and the rate of interest, and the customer's signature will have to be in a special box on the form of agreement, which must also contain the following warning, printed in a red box: 'This is a Credit Agreement regulated by the Consumer Credit Act 1974. Sign it only if you want to be legally bound by its terms.' The signature of debtor and the date of signature is appended.

Basically, the customer's rights of cancellation and so on are the same as under a hire purchase agreement.

Guaranteeing a Credit Agreement

This branch of the law is very technical, but being a surety is a risky business, even though sureties are protected to a limited degree.

Someone who obtains goods on credit may be asked to provide a guarantor – that is, a third person who agrees to make good any obligations incurred under the terms of the credit agreement. Guarantees are frequently called for where the customer is not considered a good risk by the finance company. Sureties of this sort all into two groups in law – 'guarantee' and 'indemnities'. The difference between a guarantee and an indemnity is straightforward: under a guarantee the guarantor is only liable if the debtor defaults, but an indemnity is a promise to pay in any event, so that the finance company can take direct action against a person who has signed an indemnity without involving the original debtor. An indemnity is a promise that the creditor will suffer no loss from granting the credit, and so an indemnity is fully enforceable even if the customer is under the age of eighteen. This was the ruling of the Court of Appeal in *Yeoman Credit Ltd v Latter*(1961), where Clifford Owen signed a document headed 'Hire-Purchase Indemnity and Undertaking' so as to enable Terry Latter to buy a motor-car on hire-purchase terms. Mr Latter never paid any of the instalments and the car was repossessed, and Clifford Owen was held liable. He would not have been liable if the document had been a guarantee in the legal sense.

The Consumer Credit Act 1974 now governs guarantees and indemnities and works very much in favour of the guarantor. Section 113(1) effectively reduces nearly all indemnities to the level of guarantees: (a) The guarantee or indemnity cannot allow the finance company to recover more from the surety than he would from the customer. (b) If the hire purchase or credit sale agreement is itself unenforceable, eg, because the formalities have not been complied with, the guarantee is similarly restricted. (c) Guarantees taken in relation to prospective agreements are not enforceable until the main agreement comes into effect. This means that in most cases the surety can withdraw the guarantee until that time.

Finance companies will always insist on an indemnity if the customer is under age – a young man buying a motor-cycle, for example – and recognising the special position in such cases the Act does allow indemnities to be enforced. Regulations lay down the form and content of guarantees and indemnities. There must be a signature box warning the surety that he may have to pay instead of the customer. The surety gets a copy of the agreement when it is handed or sent to him for signature.

3. Other Forms of Retail Credit

Although hire purchase and credit sales are the most common form of retail credit, a variety of other schemes are available, most of them for obtaining credit on a short-term basis. Here we deal with other types of credit transactions, all of which are subject to the Consumer Credit Act 1974.

(i) Budget Accounts

Many departments stores operate a form of revolving credit for their customers. These schemes are called by a variety of names, but broadly speaking they all operate in the same way. The customer makes regular payments into the account of a set amount each month and is given a 'credit limit', which is usually 12 or 24 times the monthly payment. So if a customer agrees to pay £20 each month he will be given a 'credit limit' of £240 or £480 and is then allowed to charge his purchases to the account, up to the credit limit. How much credit is available at any time depends on how much the customer has charged to the account and how much he has paid in.

This is an expensive form of credit. A charge is almost invariably made for the facility, either by way of interest on the amount outstanding or on the basis of the value of purchases made during the previous three months.

Some large groups of retail stores operate these schemes themselves, in which case the credit contract is a standing offer to supply goods on the instalment terms set out in the terms and conditions, and each sale is a credit sale. In others cases, the credit will be supplied by a separate company. The 1974 Act describes this sort of transaction as 'running-account credit'. The customer's legal rights in respect of goods bought on a budget account are exactly the same as those in a straightforward sale of goods transaction.

(ii) Budget Option Accounts

This is a variant of the budget account, and such schemes are usually operated by a specialist company, which is either independent or set up by the retailer for this purpose. Once again, a credit limit is given. This is not based on the amount of repayment but on the company's assessment of the credit risk. The usual credit limit varies from £350 to £1,500. The customer has the option of paying the account in (without interest) or of taking extended credit and paying a specified minimum monthly sum and becoming liable to interest on the balance. The minimum amount payable will be set out on the statement and this is once again a very expensive form of credit. The customer's rights in respect of goods purchased are again identical to his rights under an ordinary sale of goods transaction which, indeed, the purchase is.

(iii) Credit Cards

Credit cards are commonly known as 'plastic money' and enable the customer to make purchases without having to carry cash. They may be issued by a bank, eg, a Barclaycard, or by a credit-card company, and in both cases the customer has legal protection under the Consumer Credit Act 1974 and has rights against the credit-card company if the goods or services purchased with the card are unsatisfactory. This operates very much in the customer's favour. Two different types of facility are offered.

(A) Travel and entertainment cards. American Express and Diner's Club are typical travel and entertainment cards. They allow credit on a short-term basis since the entire current debt must be cleared once a month. The customer has no pre-fixed credit limit, although retailers and so on who participate in the scheme may have a 'floor limit' set by the credit card company which means that if the customer wished to purchase above that limit, the retailer will telephone the credit card company for authorisation. Cards of this type are a useful alternative to cash and can be used world-wide. The credit card company makes very searching inquiries about an applicant's credit worthiness before issuing the card, for which it makes an annual charge. The credit-card company is not liable for the quality of goods or service which are bought with the card and the customer's redress is against the supplier of the goods or services.

By signing the card the card holder becomes responsible for it and is bound by the Conditions of Use. If the card is stolen or misused, so long as the customer has acted properly, his liability is limited to £30 under sections 83 and 84 of the Consumer Credit Act 1974. The Conditions of Use form the basis of the contract between the card holder and the credit card company and should be read and understood. Typically, the conditions provide as follows:

(a) Only the card holder is authorised to use the card;

(b) The card can only be used during its period of validity – usually two years from date of issue;

(c) Statements must be settled in full on receipt. A period of grace for payment is usually allowed – 40 days after statement date is common – and if payment is not made in full by that date a default or service charge is added;

(d) If the card is lost or stolen, the card holder must inform the credit card company immediately. There is usually a charge of £5 for a replacement card;

(e) The card company has the right to stop the customer's use of the card by telling suppliers not to accept it;

(f) The card remains the credit company's property and must be returned on demand;

(g) 'Diners Club is not responsible for the standard, quality or suitability of any goods, tickets or services purchases with the card; all statements must be paid in full and without set-off or counterclaim. This does not, however, affect any statutory rights which you may have as a consumer or your rights against the [supplier] with whom all claims should be settled direct. Diners Club is not responsible if any [supplier] refuses to accept the card';

(h) The rules may be changed by the credit card company notifying the card holder to that effect.

Credit card application form

As explained in the text, the application form is the basis of the contract between you and the credit card company.

The form must be fully completed in every respect:

* The company may require further information from you.
* The company will certainly make credit checks and take up references.
* Some companies seek details of your outgoings as well.
* County Court judgments registered against you or even non-payment of a debt may disqualify you as you are then a bad credit risk.
* Although the company is not bound to give you any reason for refusing to issue the card, it must, if asked by you, give you details of any credit reference agency used.
* The credit card company is seeking to establish that you are a stable credit risk; hence the questions about length of occupancy of your home and the number of years have have been with your employer.

(B) Ordinary credit cards. In contrast to travel and entertainment type cards are credit cards such as Barclaycard, Visa and Access. Technically, they are 'credit token agreements' and are covered by section 14 of the Consumer Credit Act 1974. Their main function is to allow the customer to obtain goods or services from suppliers which have arrangements with the credit card company, and the important point about cards of these types is that anything the customer buys with the card becomes a 'linked transaction', which means that the customer has equal rights against both the supplier and the credit card company. The card company is jointly liable with the supplier for a consumer purchase made with the card of a cash value between £30 and £15,000: section 75 of the 1974 Act. This is a valuable protection and, in recent years, has proved beneficial to card holders who purchased holidays or air tickets with a credit card when the holiday company or airline subsequently became insolvent.

A feature of this type of card is that the customer is given a pre-set credit limit – usually in the range of £250 to £1,500 – and may make purchases within this limit. They offer extended credit. The card holder has the option of settling the account in full on a monthly basis (in which case no credit charge is incurred) or alternatively of making a minimum payment, in which case he is charged interest on the amount due, usually at something like 22%, though this varies in accordance with the bank base rates.

The card holder is bound by the conditions of use and in all other respects the situation is the same as with travel and entertainment type cards. The customer must not overshoot his credit limit although in practice the card companies have a generous and rather optimistic outlook on this. Some of the companies will respond to over-spending by raising the credit limit! Nevertheless, deliberately to exceed the limit may be a criminal offence.

(iv) Check and Voucher Trading

There are a number of check-trading organisations and this form of credit is quite popular in the north of England. The customer buys checks or vouchers, and uses them to buy goods from stores taking part in the scheme. Each check has a face value which the customer pays to the check-trader by weekly instalments, which include a hefty premium for interest. The store accepting the check supplies the customer with goods up to its face value, and receives payment – less a substantial discount – from the check trader. The credit is for a fixed amount. There is no rebate for repaying earlier and the true rate of interest is usually about 25%. The repayment period is often 21 weeks.

Vouchers are similar, but a voucher usually has a greater face value than the check, and the amounts of credit involved are larger. Vouchers are often repayable on a monthly basis and invariably over a longer period – 100 weeks is not uncommon. No rebate is granted for early payment. In both cases, if the customer agrees to buy checks or vouchers, he must be given a copy of the written agreement, signed on the check trader's behalf, when he receives them.

If the goods are faulty or unsatisfactory the customer has the usual Sale of Goods Act rights against the supplier.

Using a credit card sensibly

Try to pay off your monthly outstanding balance in full, thus avoiding interest, which is currently about 22% with Access and Barclaycard. The interest rate is usually higher on store cards. Time your purchases correctly. The standard period of free credit is 25 days from the date of the statement. Purchases made just before or on the statement date are not normally included in the next month's statement, so giving in effect an interest-free period of 50 days or slightly more. Use your credit card for purchases of more than £100 as then the credit card company is equally liable with the supplier for defects in the goods, etc. The purchase must be between £100 and £10,000.

---

4. Regulation of Credit Business

The Consumer Credit Act 1974 regulates all those who deal in credit. Credit dealers must all have a licence from the Office of Fair Trading and the Act covers not only those who provide credit, eg, under hire purchase agreements, and credit brokers who introduce individuals to sources of credit, but also debt-adjusters, debt-counsellors and most debt-collectors. A licence is required to carry on business falling into these categories unless the credit never exceeds £30. Unlicensed trading is an offence and, in the case of a creditor (lender) or credit broker, makes any subsequent agreement unenforceable unless the Director General of Fair Trading makes an order to the contrary. Canvassing for credit away from trade premises is strictly controlled. Canvassing for debtor-creditor agreements, which are loans which are not made under an arrangement with a supplier, and credit-brokerage, debt-adjusting and debt-counselling may not be canvassed at all. Other forms of credit can be canvassed only if there is a licence. It is an offence to send circulars offering credit or about credit facilities to a minor – a person under eighteen years of age. It is also an offence to give a person a credit token (which includes a credit card) if he has not asked for it, unless of course it is a renewal under an existing agreement. A 'credit token' is not limited to a credit card. There are also restrictions on advertisements for retail credit and the 1974 Act, in an endeavour to protect people from themselves and from the 'hard-sell', has hedged the granting of credit about with numerous restriction.

5. Credit Rating and Refusal of Credit

Anyone over the age of eighteen can obtain credit, provided they are considered a good risk. The supplier (or finance house) may wish to take up references from other suppliers or the customer's bank. Most finance house also check with a credit reference agency – such as Dun and Bradstreet – to check the customer's credit rating. The agency keeps records – usually on computer – about bad payers and those who have had court judgments registered against them for debt. Anyone who has ever bought anything on credit is likely to have a file kept on him by one or other of the agencies. The information which they keep is both favourable and unfavourable.

The customer is always entitled to know what information is on file about him, whether or not credit is refused. The 1974 Act and regulations made under it require the creditor or dealer to disclose the identity of any credit reference agency consulted. This information must be supplied within seven days of a written request, which can be made within 28 days of the date when the parties last had dealings. The consumer can then write, sending a fee of £1, for a copy of his file. This must be in plain English, and must be supplied within seven days of the customer's request, along with a notice in a special form telling him of his right to have any inaccurate information corrected. If the agency has no file on the customer it must tell him so. If the customer thinks that the information is incorrect, he can give written notice requiring its removal or correction. The agency has 28 days to reply and supply him with a copy of any amended entry. If the entry has not been removed from the file, the customer has a further 28 days in which to insist that there be added to the file a note of correction which he had drafted. This cannot be more than 200 words in length. In turn, the agency has 28 days in which to tell the consumer either that it intends to comply or that it will refer the matter to the Office of Fair Trading, eg, because the correction is defamatory. The OFT will often try to act as conciliator. Inaccuracies can and do creep into credit reference agency files, and unfortunately some of these files are based on addresses rather than on individuals, and this has led in some cases to credit being refused.

Most credit application forms require the customer to give a great deal of detail about himself – his name and address, occupation, details of his employment, and whether he owns or rents property. It is a criminal offence to give false information on an application and the applicant's answers must be truthful. They are always checked out. The pitfalls of falsehood are shown by *The Crown v Webb* (1961), where Webb applied for a mortgage. He stated on the application from that he was earning £1,250 a year, whereas his real income was only £780. He also stated that he was the manager of a motor repair firm, whereas he was in fact a partner. The building society wrote to the firm for confirmation of these statements. Webb intercepted the letter, typed a fraudulent reply on the firm's notepaper and forged his partner's signature. The building society advanced money to him. Subsequently Webb was made bankrupt by another creditor. Although the building society realised the mortgage security without making a loss, Webb's activities came to light and he was prosecuted and convicted. He was jailed for six months. When seen by the police, he was alleged to have said 'I'm sure I'm not the only one who has had to boost his income to get a mortgage'. The position about false information is exactly the same under any form of credit application.

It is unlawful to discriminate against women in connection with the grant of credit just as it is to do so on the grounds of race. Discrimination means either (a) less favourable treatment or (b) imposing conditions which are harder for such applicants to meet and which cannot be shown to be justifiable.

The position is neatly illustrated by *Quinn v Williams Furniture Ltd* (1981) where Mrs Quinn applied for hire purchase. She was told that her husband must act as a guarantor. She asked twice whether she would have had to guarantee her husband's repayments and was told 'no'. Mrs Quinn had a good job, had paid over half the cash price by the way of deposit and had substantial sums in a deposit account. The Court of Appeal held that this amounted to discrimination. Lord Denning said:

'By requiring, or even suggesting or advising that she should get her husband to sign the guarantee form in order to facilitate the agreement being entered into, it seems to me that there was unlawful discrimination against Mrs Quinn'.

The remedy for unlawful discrimination is an injunction, the effect of which may be to force at the granting of credit in such cases. The discrimination is not a criminal offence.

6. Extortionate Credit Bargains

Since 1977, the courts have had power to reopen 'extortionate credit bargains' and, effectively, to vary the rate of interest where credit has been granted to an individual. This applies to all credit bargains and not merely to credit agreements regulated by the Act. The customer is given the right to challenge the agreement on the ground that it is an 'extortionate credit bargain' by applying to the Court. The power is also exercisable if, for example, the creditor is seeking to enforce the agreement. It applies to agreements 'whenever made' and the power could scarcely be wider.

No doubt many borrowers think that they are being charged an exorbitant rate of interest, but this is not same as an extortionate bargain. A bargain is only extortionate if: (a) it requires payments which are *grossly* exorbitant; or (b) it otherwise *grossly* contravenes the ordinary principles of fair dealing. The Consumer Credit Act 1974 lays down several criteria for determining whether the agreement is extortionate and in practice very few attempts to vary interest rates are successful. The criteria are very restrictive. They are:

(i) The rates of interest prevailing at the time of the agreement was made. All the factors must be taken into account. There is no rule of thumb for assessing whether interest rates are too high. A high rate of interest may be justified, for example, if the lender was the borrower's last resort because he was unable to get credit elsewhere or because he is a bad risk. The giving of security – for example a second mortgage – is also relevant. There is a tariff for most forms of credit – and a true interest rate of 48% is not uncommon in some situations – and the tariff is likely to be upheld in most cases;

(ii) The age, experience, business capacity and state of heath of the customer;

(iii) The financial pressure on the customer;

(iv) The degree of risk involved and the security available. The position is well illustrated by the case of *A. Ketley Ltd v Scott* (1980), where Mr Scott had the chance to buy his home as a sitting tenant. He failed to obtain finance before signing the contract of purchase, when he paid a deposit of £2,500 on the price of £22,500. As a last resort, since he was in danger of losing his deposit, he approached Ketleys who agreed to lend him £20,500 for a short period at an annual interest rate of 48%. The Court ruled that this was not an 'extortionate bargain' in the circumstances. The lenders were taking a big risk – the shortness of time had prevented them making proper inquiries and the loan represented a high percentage of the value of the property;

(v) The relationship of the creditor with the customer;

(vi) Other relevant factors.

Even if the credit bargain is found to be extortionate, the Court will not necessarily reopen it. For example, if the customer has not disclosed information about himself which shows that he is a bad risk the Court would refuse to intervene. But if the customer's challenge is successful, the creditor cannot proceed to judgment against him, and the Court has power to alter the terms of the agreement.

7. Rates of Interest – Calculating the Annual Percentage Rate

Interest rate are misleading. Most customers are concerned with how much they have to repay a month and in the past lenders did not have to provide customers with the rate of interest. Now they must do so. The customer must be given:

(A) An accurate percentage rate.
Flat rates are inaccurate. A flat rate is the monthly or annual rate of interest but this is not the same as the true rate of interest. If a man borrows £100 repayable over a year at a flat rate of 10% in monthly instalments, each instalment reduces the debt. A true rate of interest is almost 20% because, in the example, the debt averaged out over twelve months is about £55. A rough and ready calculation for finding the true rate is to multiply the flat by a factor of 1.8, but more accurate figures can be obtained by more sophisticated calculations.

(B) A common comparison or yardstick, which is what the debtor who pays annually would pay.
The end result is called the Annual Percentage Rate – APR – and this is what must be stated. There are very complicated rules for working out the APR.

Bank Accounts

Today's consumer is faced with a bewildering choice of banking facilities. These range from the traditional 'current account' or cheque account operated by the 'clearing banks' to what are effectively deposit accounts (on which interest is paid) which include a facility to draw cheques. Banking facilities are offered not only by the traditional banks but also by building societies, finance houses, and National Giro which is a special bank run by the Post Office. Competition is fierce, and the services provided are similar. All of these institutions hold their customers' money, make regular payments on customers' behalf by 'standing order', and enable payments to be made by the customer to third parties. Some of the institutions offer other facilities as well: they provide foreign currency or travellers' cheques for use abroad, and offer advice on investments, stocks and shares and insurance. In many cases they offer loans or overdrafts as a means of raising finance.

1. Types of Account

(i) Current Account
A current account gives the customer a chequebook which enables him to withdraw money from his account at any time, either by making out a cheque to 'cash' or by making it payable to someone else. A cheque is the customer's written instruction to the bank requiring payment to be made. The bank will also arrange periodical payments to third parties by standing order and direct debit, both based on the customer's written instructions. Current account customers may also be able to arrange to borrow money by way of an overdraft or a bank loan.

Until recently, most current accounts were operated by the 'clearing banks' of which Barclays, Lloyds, National Westminster, and Midland are the best known – who collect payments for cheques paid in through the London Bankers' Clearing House. Nowadays they face stiff competition from other financial institutions and it pays to shop around. The main advantage of an account with one of the major clearing banks is that they have branches in most towns and cities throughout the country, whereas some of the competing institutions have very few branches. All the major clearing banks also offer a 'cash card' facility through which the customer can withdraw money from automatic machines when the bank is closed, including evenings and weekends. The clearing banks' short opening hours – 9.30am to 3.30 pm on five days a week – have been a prime reason for the growing competition from other deposit takers, although some of the big clearing banks are now reversing their policy against Saturday opening (when most people want to use the bank) by opening branches for short periods on Saturday mornings.

Current accounts may also be opened with other financial institutions, and sometimes these accounts offer significant advantages. A recent innovation is a package offered by a number of banks which combines:

(a) A current account with no charges and no minimum balance requirement;

(b) A borrowing option, often called the credit limit option, under which the bank offers a pre-arranged credit facility up to a given amount. Some of these accounts also cater for customers who occasionally overdraw without realising it, eg because a payment into the account has been delayed, and allow the customer to overdraw a small sum for a few days without special prior arrangement;

(c) A savings option, providing for automatic transfers to deposit account where the money will earn interest;

(d) In some cases, the package includes payment of interest on balances in the current account as well as no charges, though to qualify there is sometimes a minimum balance requirement or a differential rate of interest, depending on the amount involved. The various schemes on offer should be carefully compared, as to conditions and restrictions and certainly the non-clearing bankers usually require more information about a prospective customer and his financial commitments than do the 'high street banks'.

(ii) Cheque Guarantee Cards

An important facility offered with most current accounts is a *cheque card* which gives a guarantee by the bank that any cheque supported by the card will be met by the bank, even if the customer has insufficient funds in his current account. Cheque cards are not credit cards. They are a promise by the bank to pay the supplier who accepts a cheque backed by the card that it will be duly honoured provided it does not exceed a certain amount. The current limit imposed by most banks is £50, although one or two banks issue cheque cards for greater amounts. Barclaycards – although primarily credit cards – also function as cheque cards.

Before a customer can be given a cheque card by his bank he must enter into an agreement with the bank authorising it to meet cheques backed by the card. A payment by cheque with a cheque card cannot be countermanded except in case of fraud, and the customer's undertakings to the bank are extensive. The cheque card also has conditions printed on its back, and the bank will only meet the cheque if those conditions are observed. The standard conditions are as follows: (a) The cheque must be signed in the presence of the payee and the signature must correspond to that on the cheque card; (b) The cheque is drawn on a bank cheque bearing the code number of the card; (c) The cheque must be dated before the expiry date of the card; (d) The payee must write the card number on the back of the cheque. It is not sufficient if the customer writes the number; the person in whose favour the cheque is drawn (or someone authorised on his behalf) must write the number on the back on the cheque.

(iii) Payment by Cheque

Apart from small items, most consumer purchases are paid by cheque. Cheques are either 'crossed' or 'uncrossed', and the practical difference is that a crossed cheque can only be paid into another bank account whereas an uncrossed cheque can be exchanged for cash. Crossing a cheque is a protection against fraud.

The relationship between a bank and its customer is based on contract. The main terms of the contract are that the bank will honour its customer's cheques – which are an instruction to the bank to pay – provided there is sufficient money in the account or an overdraft facility has been agreed, and that the bank will maintain its customer's confidences. It must not disclose details of his financial position or dealings to anyone else without the customer's authority which can, of course, be given where the customers give the bank's name as a reference.

Sometimes a cheque will be dishonoured or, to use a popular expression, 'bounced'. The bank is only entitled to dishonour a customer's cheque on very limited grounds.

(A) If there are insufficient cleared funds in the account and there is no agreed overdraft limit. All banks reserve the right to withhold payment of cheques drawn against what are called 'uncleared effects', which are payments in by cheque which have not been cleared through the clearing house system. So, if the customer pays a cheque into his account on Monday, he should not draw cheques against its value for several days – it takes at least three working days to 'clear' a cheque through the system. Although the account may be credited with the amount of the in-payment, the bank still has the right to refuse to pay against the sum credited until it is cleared. Similarly, if there are insufficient cleared funds in the account to meet the value of a cheque drawn, the bank can bounce the cheque, just as it can where to pay it would exceed any overdraft limit previously agreed.

(B) Where there is a mistake on the cheque – for example, if the customer has forgotten to sign or date it or some other discrepancy. A common mistake is for the words and figures to differ.

Banks use different terms when dishonouring cheques – they are returned to the collecting banker and the matter is then between the customer and the payee. A cheque can be 'stopped' by the customer in certain circumstances (see below). A cheque can, therefore, be dishonoured for a number of reasons, and to have a cheque 'bounced' can cause serious embarrassment and difficulty to the customer. Banks frequently make mistakes, but the private customer is in a difficult position. Although by wrongfully bouncing a cheque the bank is in breach of contract, the customer's only entitlement would to be a pound or two by way of nominal damages.

This is shown in the case *Gibbons v Westminster Bank Ltd* (1939), where the bank wrongfully dishonoured a cheque drawn by Mrs Gibbons in payment of her rent. The mistake was entirely the bank's since Mrs Gibbons had paid in more than sufficient to meet the cheque; the payment had been credited to the wrong account. As a result, the landlords insisted that all future payments of rent be made by cash and not by cheque. Although the bank was liable, Mrs Gibbons was held entitled to recover only nominal damages of £2. The position would have been different if Mrs Gibbons could have proved that she suffered some specific financial loss.

The position is different in the case of a business account. A trader whose cheque is wrongfully dishonoured is entitled to recover substantial damages – often many hundreds of pounds – and in an extreme case a tradesman might be able to recover damages from the bank for defamation of character (libel).

The rights of the payee of a dishonoured cheque are well protected by law. If the cheque is dishonoured for technical reasons, or because it is marked 'Refer to drawer: please represent' or 'Effects not cleared' most people simply represent the cheque for payment and, indeed, it is banking practice to do this. However, as the Court of Appeal has pointed out, a cheque is for all practical purposes 'to be treated as cash; it is to be honoured unless there is some good reason to the contrary' (Lord Denning in *Fielding & Platt v Najjar* (1969) and one result is that the payee has an independent right to sue on the cheque as opposed to the transaction to which it relates.

In some cases the customer has the right to 'stop' a cheque – that is, to instruct the bank not to pay it. A cheque backed by a cheque card cannot be 'stopped'. Where a cheque is stopped, the bank will mark it 'orders not to pay'. A stop can be put on a cheque by telephone, but the bank will insist on having written confirmation giving the number of the cheque, its date and details of the payee and the amount.

A buyer should not stop the cheque because he has decided that after all he does not like the goods. Although the instruction to the bank not to pay will be effective to stop the cheque, it will be a breach of both the contract of sale and of the seller's rights under the cheque. Even if, as between buyer and seller, the customer is entitled to stop the cheque, he may find that he is under some liability to a third party who took the cheque in good faith. Furthermore, if a cheque is wrongfully stopped, and it can be proved that the customer had no intention of paying for the goods, he may be subject to a criminal prosecution. Where the customer knows that he is expected to pay on the spot for goods supplied to him or services rendered to him it is an offence for him dishonestly to go away without having paid and never intending to pay.

It is a criminal offence, punishable by imprisonment, to write out a cheque knowing that the bank is unlikely to meet it and, indeed, anyone who 'bounces' a cheque may find himself subject to prosecution for obtaining a financial advantage by deception. Misuse of a cheque card is similarly an offence.

A cheque is 'negotiable' – that is, it can be transferred to third parties by being endorsed over by the payee – and the third party who takes the cheque in good faith and for value has direct rights against the drawer. So, if the payee has endorsed the cheque to an innocent third party, the endorsee will be entitled to sue on the cheque.

Payment by cheque is not complete until the cheque is actually delivered, and until then the risk of misappropriation is on the customer as between himself and a seller of goods. Cheques may be lost or stolen and then misused. Sometimes the customer loses his cheque book or it may be stolen, and a wrongdoer manages to obtain money by using it. Provided the customer has not been negligent, it is the bank which bears the loss. Cheque books are valuable documents and should be kept carefully – the customer must take reasonable care. It is not taking reasonable care to sign a blank cheque or to write it in such a way that the figures can be easily altered. All cheque books have a series of warnings printed on their inside front cover. These warnings include instructions to prevent fraud. The amount of the cheque, in words and figures should begin as far as possible over to the left of the space provided so that no other word and figures can be inserted. Any alterations should be confirmed with the customer's full signature. Cheque books and cheque cards should not be kept together – this facilitates fraud.

(iv) Budget Accounts

A budget account is a variant of the current account which enables the customer to spread his expenses over the year by regular payments. It is a current account with a built-in overdraft facility. The customer agrees with the bank the total of his likely regular expenses for the year – mortgage payments, rates, heating and lighting, telephone and so on – and signs a standing order transferring a fixed sum of money from his current account to his budget account each month – the total of the agreed expenses plus a charge, divided by twelve. The bank then gives him a special cheque book and the customer can overdraw on the account when several bills arrive at the same time. The budget account is a means of spreading payments over the whole year, and is otherwise subject to the same rules as an ordinary current account.

(v) *Loan Accounts*
Banks are in the business of lending money and will make loans to fiance a customer's purchase from a dealer or for other purposes. Such loans – repayable by instalments over a fixed period, which may be up to five years – are 'consumer credit agreements' if they do not exceed £15,000 and are then subject to the provisions of the Consumer Credit Act 1974, including all its formalities, including warning boxes, supply of copies of the agreement, and so on. Perhaps unintentionally, the 1974 Act has made borrowing from a bank more complicated – though overdraft arrangements are not caught by the 1974 Act.

(vi) *Deposit Accounts*
A deposit account is one form of savings account. The customer puts money on deposit with the bank, and receives interest in return. The rate of interest varies according to bank rate. Usually, seven days' notice to withdraw money is required – though the exact details vary from bank to bank – and a higher rate of interest may be obtained by keeping large sums in the account. Savings accounts are a variant of the ordinary deposit account – the customer agrees to pay in a regular sum each month – and the accumulated balance earns interest.

2. Bank Giro

The banks run a credit-transfer system – called bank giro – which is an alternative to paying bills by cheque. The customer fills out a special form for each firm he wants to pay – many major concerns print standard forms on their accounts – and hand them to the bank with the total amount in cash or by cheque. Several bills can be paid at the same time using one cheque. A similar service is operated through the National Girobank (the Post Office bank) and is called Transcash.

Debts and Financial Problems

More and more people are getting into debt, often because they take on commitments which they cannot really afford. In other cases disaster strikes because someone loses his job, and finds that on a depleted income he cannot pay bills which he has run up. If this happens, all is not lost because creditors only take legal action as a last resort.

When someone runs into difficulties, the first step is to inform the creditor as soon as possible. This applies whether it is an unpaid bill, a hire-purchase agreement, or any form of credit. In practice, most creditors will adopt a sympathetic approach, and accept payments by instalments or over a longer period. The essential point is that the debtor should be frank and explain his difficulties and make realistic proposals and keep to them.

Unless the debtor acts sensibly in this way, the creditor is going to take a strong line and, unless the amount involved is very small, will attempt to recover the money. Very small debts may, in practice be written off, but it would be rash to assume that this will happen. Both tradesmen and lending institutions have their own procedures for recovering debts due to them.

1. Debt Collecting Agencies

Debt collecting agencies need a licence from the Director-General of Fair Trading. Operating as a debt-collector without a licence is a criminal offence. The agencies usually operate on a commission basis, and the larger agencies have local agents throughout the country. Sometimes they send someone to call on the debtor, but more usually they start off by writing to him on the creditor's behalf.

Debt collectors have no special legal status, and both they (and the creditor) can only attempt to collect the debt by legal means. It is a criminal offence to harass a debtor by making frequent or threatening demands for payment, and there are various controls:
(i) Neither the creditor nor the collector must ask for payment in such a way as to indicate that they are acting in an official capacity, eg, as a Court official, and amongst other things they are not allowed to send demands which look as though they are official Court forms.

(ii) They must not harass or bully the debtor so as to subject him or his family to alarm, humiliation or distress. This means, for example, that shops cannot display 'shame list' of debtors – though there is nothing to prevent trade organisations from exchanging lists of debtors amongst themselves or advising their members of bad debtors and this happens frequently in practice. Any debtor who thinks he is being harassed should report the matter to the police. A typical case of harassment would be parking a van marked 'Debt Collector' outside the debtor's front door. The majority of debt-collecting agencies are reputable and responsible, and it may be possible to make arrangements even at this stage to pay off what is owed by instalments.

2. County Court Proceedings

The creditor may decide to use the Courts to recover his money. Most debt recovery proceedings are taken in the County Court which has jurisdiction where the amount claimed does not exceed £5,000 although some larger creditors – banks and hire-purchase companies, for example – may opt to start proceedings in the High Court. But the vast majority of creditors' claims for debt are disposed of in the County Courts.

The first step in the process will usually be a letter from the creditor's solicitor demanding repayment of the money. The letter will usually state that failure to pay the debt in full within a short period of time – seven to 14 days – or the making of satisfactory proposals for repayment, will result in legal proceedings. Even at this stage, creditors will often accept instalment payments, provided the debtors proposal is realistic. If the debtor owes £1,000, for example it is not realistic to offer to pay the debt off by weekly instalments of £1.

It is best to arrange to pay if this can be agreed because, if Court proceedings are started, the debtor will be liable for legal costs as well and these soon mount up. A letter offering to pay off the debt due by instalments should always include a payment on account as a token of good faith. If the debtor fails to respond to the solicitor's letter, and the creditor decides to take Court proceedings, the solicitor will go along to the Court office and issue a 'default summons', which will be sent by the Court to the debtor by post unless the solicitor arranges (for an extra fee) to have the summons served personally by a County Court bailiff. The default summons (see opposite) requires the debtor to admit or deny the claim within fourteen days. It will be accompanied by a form which the debtor must fill in and return to the Court with the fourteen day period. This form enables the debtor to make an offer to pay by instalments if he wishes, and he must then provide details of his income and outgoings.

The creditor is not bound to accept payment by instalments but once again, in practice, may well agree to do so. If he does not – for example, because he thinks the proposal is unrealistic – the case will proceed to be heard. Smaller claims are dealt with by the County Court Registrar, who may well make an order that the debt be paid by instalments which are geared to the debtor's income and commitments, but he is not bound to do. If an instalments order is made, it is essential that the instalments are made promptly to the County Court office as specified in the order. Payments have to be made in cash or by cheque (backed by a cheque guarantee card) at the Court office, or they may be made by post, using postal orders or cash (sent by registered post). The Court will not accept cheque payments by post.

Where a debt is disputed, the Court proceedings will be held in public and there will be a trial. But if the debt is admitted, and the creditor is merely disputing the question of repayment, there will be a private hearing 'in chambers'. The Court will fix a date for this hearing – called 'the disposal date' – and the debtor must turn up then, taking with him evidence of his means. The registrar will hear what the parties have to say, there will be questions asked, and then he will decide the method of payments and make the order.

3. Enforcing a Judgment

When the debtor refuses to pay, or ignores the Court order, the consequences are drastic. There are several ways open to the creditor to enforce his judgment and recover his money from the debtor. Only in a very few cases will it not be worth the creditor's while to enforce the judgment, for example, if the debtor has moved on and left no forwarding address. Even in these cases, however, if a substantial sum is involved, a larger creditor will undoubtedly make strenuous efforts to trace the defaulter.

The consequences of failure to pay a judgment debt are unpleasant, the last resort being that the debtor can be made bankrupt.

(i) Seizing the Debtor's Goods
The most common form of enforcing a judgment is by 'levying execution' against the debtor's goods, which means putting the bailiffs in. The debtor's goods are seized by the bailiffs and then sold to pay off what is due. This method is available both for the whole amount and where there are instalments outstanding. The creditor applies to the Court to issue a 'warrant of execution' – a fee is payable, depending on the amount involved. The debtor is informed when the warrant is issued and then has a further seven days in which to pay up. He can also pay the bailiff when he calls.

Alternatively, the debtor can apply to the Court to suspend the warrant, and even at this stage the Court may do so (after a hearing) and make an order for payments by instalments. But the Court is unlikely to suspend a warrant on more than one occasion.

Often the mere issue of the warrant is enough to make the debtor pay up, but if he does not do so – or take one of the other actions outlined – the bailiffs will enter his house and seize goods to the value of the warrant. The trouble with this method of enforcement – from the creditor's point of view – is that when the goods are sold by auction they usually fetch very little.

The bailiff cannot take the debtor's own clothes, bedding or the tools of his trade up to a value of £250, but can take anything else which belongs to the debtor. He cannot seize goods which belong to the debtor's family, or which are on hire- purchase or rental. The seized property is then valued and auctioned and, after the (heavy) expenses involved have been deducted, the creditor gets the balance.

In some cases the bailiffs will take what is called 'walking possession'. He lists the property seized and asks the debtor to sign a form agreeing not dispose of the listed goods and leaves the goods behind.

(ii) Deductions from Earnings

The debtor can apply to the Court for an attachment of earnings order which requires the employer to make regular deductions from his wages or salary to satisfy the judgment. The employer pays the money to the Court which in turn pays it to the creditor. This method can only be used if the debtor has a regular job and not if he self-employed. If the creditor applies to the Court for an attachment of earning order, the debtor is informed and must give the Court full details of his income, outgoings and other relevant facts. The Registrar then decides how much the debtor can afford to pay. If the debtor changes his job, he must inform the Court within seven days, because the attachment order lapses and a fresh one must be made.

When an order is made a 'protected earnings figure' is specified, and the employer does not make a deduction if the debtor's earnings fall below this figure.

(iii) Garnishee Order

Another method of enforcing a judgment is a 'garnishee order' which is useful where the debtor is in business and is owed money by others or has money in his bank account. To get this information, it is usual for the creditor to apply to the Court for an inquiry into the debtor's means. A hearing is held at which the debtor must answer questions put to him about his assets and liabilities. If it emerges that he is owed money, the creditor asks the Court for a garnishee order requiring the third party who owes money to the debtor in the ordinary course of business to pay the amount direct to the creditor.

If a judgment debt is unpaid – or the debtor falls behind with an instalment order – the creditor can, if he wishes, issue a judgment summons requiring the debtor to appear before the Court to give an explanation of why he has not paid. In many instances, the likely result will be a variation of the original order.

4. Administration Order

The debtor may himself apply to the Court for an adminstration order to be made the effect which is to help him organise his financial affairs. This is useful technique where the debtor has got into financial problems and has several judgment debts against him, and his total debts do not exceed £5000. Only the debtor can apply for an administration order. If it is made, the Court will decide the amounts to be paid to each creditor by instalments.

5. Bankruptcy

Bankruptcy is the ultimate method of enforcing a judgment but is definitely the last resort, though it is widely used by the Inland Revenue against people who owe arrears of income tax, as well as by the Customs and Excise in respect of unpaid value added tax. It has a number of disadvantages from the creditor's point of view – notably that fact that if, as is usual, several people are owed money, there is usually very little left to share out amongst the general body of creditors because certain creditors – such as the Inland Revenue – get preferential treatment and are paid before others, and the costs of the procedure are enormous.

The bankruptcy laws were first shaped in the 19th century. The law is now contained in the Insolvency Act 1986. The practical effect of being made bankrupt is that the bankrupt loses his property and assets which are sold and the proceeds are distributed amongst the creditors.

The purpose of bankruptcy is twofold: (a) To ensure equal distribution of assets amongst the creditors – but this is subject to an 'order of preference' and in most cases the ordinary creditors only get a few pence of each pound they are owed; and (b) to protect the debtor from the pressing demands of his creditors and to allow him to wipe the slate clean. This is the theory; the practice is very different, and attitudes are still coloured to a large extent by the residual feeling towards bankrupts which was common in the world of Mr. Micawber and 19th-century debtor's prisons. Bankruptcy laws are quasi-criminal in their operation and the undischarged bankrupt is subject to a number of serious disabilities.

Part 2 The Law and Your Leisure

Gambling

1. Introduction

Historians have traced the habit of gambling right back to the dawn of human history. The desire to stake money on the uncertain outcome of a future event which is beyond the participant's direct control is clearly a deep-rooted one. What is also clear is that laws, designed to restrict, control or even prohibit certain forms of gambling have an equally ancient lineage.

The justifications put forward for some legal limitations on gambling activity vary from the moral, through the practical, to social and economic reasons. Despite the absence of any Biblical injunction against gambling, the Church has always regarded the idea of making profit out of the inevitable loss and suffering occasional to others as the antithesis of love of one's neighbour. Even putting aside religious considerations, political leaders usually speak of gambling in disapproving tones – like Benjamin Disraeli's description of it as 'a vast engine of demoralization', or the young Harold Wilson's description of the newly introduced Premium Bonds as a 'squalid raffle'. More practical reasons motivated the Unlawful Games Act 1541 – there the object was to enable archery to be practised more regularly.

The present legal rules relating to betting, gaming and lotteries no longer seek to direct potential gamblers toward alternative pursuits. Though certain authorities would still detect in the legal rules some elements of moral disapproval of the activity as a whole, the aim of the law today (it is said) is to interfere as little as possible with individual liberty to take part in the various forms of gambling, but to impose some restrictions in order to discourage excess, and to ensure that participants in gambling (be it football pools, betting, gaming or lotteries) are not in any way defrauded.

Regulation of gambling also assists in the task of ensuring that gambling does not become an inordinate source of profit for the criminal elements in our society; the cynical observer would probably add that such regulation also allows the State to take its share of the profit accruing; in the form of taxes or duties.

2. Some Basic Principles

(i) Gambling Activities Which Are Subject to Control

Gambling may be taken to mean betting on a future event or the placing of stakes in money on such future event the outcome of which is uncertain and beyond the direct power or control of the person making the bet. Such a wide definition might include investment on the Stock Exchange or certain items of insurance – but in such circumstances any gambling element is marginal and subsidiary to the activity's main aims. The law is also not concerned with private domestic gambling: it is when a commercial operator is involved seeking to make a profit from the activity that the law steps in to control and regulate.

There are three main activities subject to control and the rules regulating each differ.

(A) Gaming: This now defined as 'the playing of a game of chance for winnings in money or money's worth' and will include games such as poker and pontoon, roulette and baccarat. There are special rules for some games, such as bingo, and lotteries and football pools are excluded from gaming control and also have separate regulation.

(B) Betting: A bet is the staking of money (or other value) on an event of a doubtful issue and, for the present law, includes:-

(a) Betting on horse or dog races, including totalisator transactions;

(b) A bet with a registered pool promoter;

(c) A wager, which is a contract between two people on the outcome of a future uncertain event (or on a past event the result of which is not known). A wager will therefore include a bet on the result of the next General Election, whether it is with your friend or at your local bookmakers. The essential feature of a wager is that either side may either win or lose.

(C) Lotteries: A lottery is the distribution of prizes by lot or chance *and* the chance of winning must be secured by a payment by the participant. All such lotteries are unlawful unless conducted under provisions of the relevant Act.

Although it will be convenient to look at each area of gambling activity in turn, is important to note that the legal definitions are not precise. As a judge once remarked, Parliament has found it impossible to keep up with the enormous variety of gambling activities which has arisen from the ingenuity of gamblers and those who try to exploit them. Consequently, the legislation gives a general indication of the activity that is controlled and leaves detailed interpretation to the courts, often in the guise of local magistrates. There is also overlap between the three main areas set out above – for example, certain pool promoters, although their activity is deemed to be the taking of bets, can acquire licences from the Gaming Board of Great Britain.

(ii) Illegality and Unenforceability

The distinction between *illegality* and *unenforceability* also needs to be stressed. Some forms of gambling are inherently unlawful and penalties may be applied if they occur: lotteries which fall outside the statutory scheme and unlicensed gaming will be illegal in this sense. By way of contrast, most bets and wagers are not illegal, but the contract of gaming or wagering which comes into being when two parties agree on a bet is, and has been since 1845, void and unenforceable. Thus you can quite lawfully bet with your friend or bookmaker, but you cannot sue in a Court to recover the winnings due to you if he fails to pay up. Not all betting comes within this definition of a 'wagering contract'; bets with a totalisator or on the football pools are different because the tote or pools promoter cannot lose but will take a specified proportion of the monies received as expenses or profit. In this case, therefore, the activity is both legal, and enforceable. This means that if the Totalisator Board allow you to have a credit account and you fail to pay the bill, they can bring a legal action to recover the money due.

In practice, the wagering contract principle is not a problem, and failure to pay by a bookmaker is unlikely to occur on a valid bet (though the validity of the bet may be disputed!) A bookie who did fail to pay might well be expelled from the National Association of Bookmakers and would find renewal of his licence to operate virtually impossible.

(iii) The Systems of Control

The principal system of control is by means of licensing. *Licences* will be necessary for betting shops and to permit gaming in clubs, and are also required for all racing tracks except horse racecourses with a certificate of approval from the Horserace Betting Levy Board. Where the gambling is not done at particular premises, *registration* is usually required. Pools promoters and societies promoting public lotteries must be registered with the appropriate local authorities.

Detailed *Regulations* and *Rules*, some contained in Acts of Parliament, others in secondary legislation made by a Minister, provide the framework within which the various gambling activities operate. The result is a system of some complexity, notwithstanding the attempts to rationalize the law in 1960. It is only possible to give a general outline of the regime to which the different gambling activities are subject. Persons applying for any licence would be well advised to seek legal advice at an early stage.

3. Betting

(i) Off Course Betting

(A) Some prohibitions. Off course betting has been permitted in licensed betting offices since 1960, but outside betting shops clear prohibitions remain. Thus:

(1) It is an offence to use any premises for the purposes of betting unless the premises are licensed, or are an approved racecourse or licensed track – maximum fine on 'standard scale' 3, currently £400.

(2) It is an offence to use any street or public place, or to loiter in streets, for the purposes of betting, bookmaking or receiving or settling bets. Maximum fine here not exceeding standard scale 4, currently £1,000. 'Street or public place' will include any place to which the public has access and will include, for example, subways, alleys, even a railway carriage, while being used for carrying passengers. Doorways and entrances of premises are included too if they abut onto a street.

(3) Betting with a person under the age of 18 continues to be prohibited, provided the young person is 'apparently' under 18 or the offender knows or ought to know that person is under age. Maximum penalty here is on the level of standard scale 5, currently £2,000.

These restrictions mean that the only legal off course betting allowed is either in or through licensed betting shops, or by post, since the sending of ready money bets in the mail has been lawful since 1960.

(B) Betting shop licensing. A betting shop can only operate lawfully if it is granted a betting office licence, which is subject to annual renewal. Application is made to the betting licensing committee of the local magistrates; and only the Totalisator Board, the holder of a bookmaker's permit, or a person credited by a bookmaker and the holder of a betting agency permit can apply for a licence. Application must be in a specified form with notice being given to the chief officer of police, the local authority and the local Customs and Excise Office. The application must be advertised in a local newspaper allowing fourteen days for objections to be sent to the clerk to the justices. Notices must be posted outside the proposed premises for the two week minimum period.

At the hearing of the licensing application objectors may be heard; the licence can be granted or refused after the hearing of the evidence. In a few circumstances the application must be refused (for example, if the premises are not enclosed; there are more general grounds of 'Unsuitability of the premises' or 'inexpediency' on which the licence may, in the magistrate's discretion, be refused. If, for example, the magistrates consider that there are already sufficient betting shops to meet the demand, they could decline to grant a licence. It should be noted that planning permission for a betting shop will be required before an application for a licence can proceed.

There is a right of appeal against the refusal to grant a licence. The reasons for which a renewal of a licence can be refused are the same as those which apply to the original grant of a licence.

(C) Management of betting shops. Since their establishment in 1960, there have always been rules regulating the internal management of betting shops. Until recently, the prohibition of advertising outside a betting shop and restrictions on the provision of television broadcasts and refreshments meant the betting shop was an austere place. As a judge remarked, the clear intention of Parliament was that these establishments should be difficult to find and, when found, should be internally as dreary as possible. Recently however (1984) the statute was amended to allow the Secretary of State to make regulations permitting the provision of refreshments (but no alcoholic liquor) and allow the broadcasting of live sound and television transmissions or video recordings. These fresh regulations were brought into force in early 1986. Detailed restrictions still remain however. A betting shop cannot open on Sundays, Good Friday or Christmas Day and on other days cannot open before 7am and must close before 6.30pm. The proprietor's betting office licence, his rules of betting and a notice prohibiting the admission of persons under the age of eighteen must all be clearly displayed. There are still strict limits on advertising the business outside premises, though the latest regulation give a slightly greater degree of freedom and the old prohibition of the display of other written advertisements and signs no longer applies. Patrons of a betting office cannot be encouraged to bet either by the proprietor or any one acting on his behalf.

(ii) On Course Betting – Horseracing

On course betting, which in terms of money staked means mainly horseracing and dogtracks, has a long social history. Such activity (especially in the case of horseracing) has not attracted the same opposition or restriction in the past as other forms of gambling. This may in part be due to the participation by all sections of society. Certainly the breeding and training of good horses was once a vital military and economic activity to which horseracing – and consequent betting – was a logical consequence. Now horseracing is a premier sporting activity despite the demise of the horse in a mechanised and technological society, and the patronage of racing by the Royal Family by the training of horses and attendance, ensures a status for horseracing unequalled for other forms of gambling.

When the law relating to betting and gaming was radically overhauled in 1960, organised horseracing was largely excluded from the provision of the legislation relating to betting. This does not mean, however, that there is not control – quite the contrary.

First, though any horserace is lawful in itself, the legal restrictions preventing the use of premises for betting or bookmaking on racecourses will apply *unless* the racecourse is an 'approved race course' used on the day in question solely for horseracing. Such approval is only given if a certificate is issued by the Horserace Betting Levy Board (The 'HBLB'). Secondly, in practice all such approved racecourses are under the effective control of the Jockey Club, which has been incorporated by royal charter.

Exclusion from the more general rules of control was therefore allowed because it was thought that the control which the Jockey Club has long exercised (formerly in association with the National Hunt Committee) was adequate to ensure the good management of racecourses.

A further reason that horseracing and its attendant gambling has always escaped from close restriction is that it is, by its nature, an occasional rather than a regular activity. In its detailed rules for the management of courses, the Jockey Club does have powers to limit the number of race meetings – and bookmakers and the public makers of bets are both subject to the discipline of the club and what is called the 'Committee of Tattersalls'. This is a semi-official body dealing with betting disputes. Its decisions are invariably observed, even though not enforceable by Court action.

A punter at a racecourse will have the choice of two main forms of betting, (i) with a bookmaker offering known odds; or (ii) with the 'tote' – the totalisator pool organised by the Horserace Totalisator Board (the 'HTB'). A bookie's odds will, of course, fluctuate from time to time in response to the support – or lack of it – for a particular runner. The punter will know in advance from the odds offered and accepted the amount he can expect in the event of a win.

The tote is a form of pool betting (see below) under the exclusive control of the HTB in which all money staked on the various chances is accumulated; and after the race there will be a specified deduction for expenses and the levy and the balance shared among the winning tickets. The punter will not know the final odds until the time for bets to close. On the face of it, the tote looks 'safer' in that it does not qualify as a 'gaming contract', discussed above, and is therefore enforceable. In practice, all bookies will also pay up, for if they fail to do so they may well find themselves excluded from all racecourses under Jockey Club rules for failing to pay or settle betting losses.

The Horseracing Betting Levy Board imposes a levy on bookmakers and the tote (via the HTB): and the money so collected is devoted to the advancement and improvement of horse breeding and racing. Through this levy, the HBLB has a measure of control over horseracing in general.

(iii) On Course Betting – Dog Racing and Other Licensed Tracks

Apart from horseracing, on course betting can only take place a 'licensed track': though this will include both betting at donkey derbies and (at the other end of social acceptability) hare coursing, in practice the rules are only relevant to dog tracks. Indeed, when compared with horseracing, (in terms of money staked on off course betting, if not in television coverage) greyhound racing might claim to be the premier sport.

The licensing of dog tracks is a function of the relevant local authority; and the exact procedure is a complex one which need not concern us, save to note that, like application for a betting shop licence, plenty of time and a considerable number of notices and advertisements are required and there are provision for objections to be heard. The licensing authority, in this case, usually a committee of the local council, has a discretion to refuse a licence which is requested. The acquisition of a track licence is likely to be a major undertaking, invariably requiring legal advice and representation; but once granted it remains in force for seven years, unless revoked.

The law prohibits racing on a licensed track on Sundays, Good Friday and Christmas Day; and the former '104 days in the year' limit was raised in 1971 for dog tracks to 130 days in any year. Gambling at such tracks will, as in the case of horseracing, be either by a totalisator pool or with a bookmaker:

(1) The licensed dog track operator has the right to install his own tote – a right which is always exercised. The establishment and operation of such a tote is subject to detailed rules; so an accountant and mechanician (this is the word that the statute uses for a technical advisor) must be appointed to inspect and examine the machine and the accounts to ensure punters are paid their due. In particular, a track operator cannot maximise his tote taking by excluding bookmakers; indeed he is under a duty to admit them and provide space for them to operate. However, the bookmaker's right of entry is not absolute or unlimited. Thus, in one case, the track operator limited the number of bookmakers he would admit to 5 to ensure the economic viability of the track and the Court upheld this limitation.

(2) The track bookmakers must be independent of the track operator – it is an offence for the operator to engage in bookmaking on his own track, and he is limited in the admission charge he can make to such bookies (5 times the charge for public admission).

It follows from the above that betting at the fighting or baiting of any animal (dogs, badgers, bears, cocks, or whatever) is unlawful. It may also be an offence of cruelty: badgers are especially protected under the Badgers Act. There are additional offences of holding or attending events where animals are fought or baited.

(iv) Pool Betting, Especially Football Pools
Pool betting has similarities to both bets at fixed odds and lotteries and it is lawful if conducted by registered pools promoters. In commercial terms, pool betting is in practice almost exclusively confined to football pools, but the legislation makes provision for pools betting on other events in addition to football.

The meaning of pool betting can be seen by comparison with betting at fixed odds on the one hand and lotteries on the other:

(A) Any bet which is not a bet at fixed odds will be by way of pool betting. When a bet at fixed odds is made, the punter can know at the time the amount he will win if the bet succeeds (except where the bet is linked, for example to the odds later offered just before the race begins). In pool betting, however, his winnings (if any) will be a share of the stake money paid and will often be divisible with other persons similarly entitled as winners. Thus eight scoring draws on the pools may produce a jackpot payout for one person: a dozen such draws will see the pool shared among many more winners.

(B) Like a lottery, pool betting is based on the principle that number of entrants make a stipulated payment in advance. A lottery, however, occurs when the winners are determined by lot or chance, as in the case when a 'Prize Draw' is made. In the case pools betting, entries comprise a forecast as to the result of sporting or other events. This involves the *possibility* of the exercise of a certain element of skill in forecasting. It is enough that there is that possibility: the fact that many pool entrants have a fixed forecast each week, or choose their numbers in a random way does not invalidate a pool or turn it into a lottery.

The law requires a commercial pools promoter to be registered with the local authority of the area where the business is situated; and the following requirements must be complied with:

(a) The business must be in the form of competitions for prizes for making forecasts as to sporting or other events. 'Other events' might include the movement of stocks and shares, and at the time of writing an organisation called 'City pools' has achieved registration in East Yorkshire for such forecast.

(b) Each bet must be an entry into a particular competition.

(c) The stakes and winnings must be paid wholly in money.

(d) In each competition, the prizes must be equally available for all the bets, so that the question of which bet qualifies for the prize or prizes shall be determined solely by the relative success and accuracy of the forecast made. An entrant who wins but stakes twice as much as a similar winner will achieve twice as much by way of winnings.

(e) The total amount payable by the way of winnings shall be the total amount of the stakes in that competition, less only pool betting duty and a percentage previously determined (and notified to the accountant) which is the same for all the competitions on the same day.

Notwithstanding these basic principles, the rules of any competition may provide for slight variations, so it is wise to check the rules applicable to any competition you enter. In particular rules can provide:

(i) that winnings shall not, in the case of any bet, exceed a stated amount with the excess being shared for bets qualifying in other prizes;

(ii) that in specified circumstances one or more of the prizes shall not be paid and the amount that would have been payable be applied to increasing the amount payable to winning bets qualifying for another prize and other prizes in that competition;

(iii) for the winnings of winning bets to be increased or decreased by not more than three pence provided this is with a view to facilitating payment;

(iv) most importantly, a rule of a pools competition which completely excludes legal liability on behalf of the pools promoter has been upheld in an old case and this rule is accepted as applying to current legislation. This means, of course, that where such a rule applies you cannot sue your pools promoter in a Court for winnings you allege to be due to you. All football pools contain this 'honour clause' (which states that the transaction is binding in honour only); but the Pools Promoters Association have a procedure to investigate any claim of failure to pay or alleged irregularities: a successful complainant will be paid what he should have won.

The law requires the appointment of an independent qualified accountant which helps to ensure equitable distribution and to minimise any possibility of the insertion or substitution of coupons after the results have been made known.

If you are sending in a pools coupon, first make sure that:

1. You complete the form clearly and correctly;
2. You sign it;
3. You post it in good time. Late entries will be rejected. The Post Office is protected against claims for delayed delivery and it is no use proving you posted it. Delivery is required.
4. The alternative to posting is the collection system used by 90% of entrants. The use of collectors is supervised by the pools companies. The coupons state that the collectors are the agents of the punters, not the companies. This means that you cannot sue the company if the collector fails to ensure that your entry arrives on time. You could sue the collector if he has deprived you of a win, but he may not have the means to pay. This 'agency' clause has not been tested in the Courts; if it were, it seems likely to be upheld.

Two other forms of pool betting may be encountered:

(1) Pool betting may be conducted on race days by the Horserace Totalisator Board or by their authority at horseracing, or by the occupier of a track on a dog racecourse.

(2) Charity Pool Competitions: a registered pools promoter who obtains a certificate from the Gaming Board (he must satisfy them that he has held at least nine competitions for the financial benefit of a charitable, cultural, sporting or noncommercial society), may be licensed by the board to hold pool competitions for prizes. This provision was passed to cover competitions where the vast majority of the entrants do not make forecasts of their own. A Court decision in 1971 held such pool betting to be a lottery, and

therefore subject to lottery rules; this provision allows such licensed competition to continue as pool betting.

4. Gaming

(i) General Principles

Gaming is the staking of money in a game of chance with other players. Since 1960, the playing of any such game is not in itself unlawful, but three types of game can only be played in licensed or registered premises. They are games:

(1) which involve playing or staking against a bank (whether or not the bank is held by one of the players); or

(2) where the chances in the game are not equally favourable to all players; or

(3) where the chances lie between the player or players and some other person who is not playing, and the chances between the players and the outsider are unequal.

These rules mean that games such as whist and bridge are quite lawful, since all players have an equal chance; but pontoon or roulette are only lawful in licensed premises.

Generally, outside licensed premises:

It is unlawful to take part in any gaming in a street or public place;

It is unlawful to make a charge for participation in a game, whether by the way of a levy on the stakes or the winnings. Club subscriptions are excluded.

Two important principles maintain and uphold social tradition, so that gaming in your own home (defined as 'taking place on a domestic occasion in a private dwelling') or hostel or hall of residence is lawful – but don't charge for entry! The second exception maintains an ancient practice, so that the playing of dominoes or cribbage in public houses is permitted provided all participants are over eighteen; and gambling linked to games of skill (darts or shove ha'penny) is not caught by the legislation.

(ii) Gaming in a Casino

Casinos were permitted in 1960, and the next eight years saw an uncontrolled expansion of the activity; in 1968, a further Gaming Act sought to prevent exploitation and provide a framework for gaming in an orderly manner free from intrusion from undesirable elements. The work of the Gaming Board since 1968 has largely achieved those objectives. The number of casinos and gaming clubs is small, 121 in 1976 and 115 on 1 January 1986, compared with over 1,200 in the mid 1960s, and less than one person in every thousand will visit a casino regularly. In 1985, 1.6 billion pounds was taken as 'Drop money' (money exchanged for chips) in casinos; though much of this will be returned as winnings, it is instructive to compare this figure with the £496 million stake at bingo. It is therefore by far and away the most expensive form of gambling in which to participate because a roulette table can turn nearly every minute, perhaps with a minimum £5 (or more) stake each time.

The operation, management and profits of casino operators are closely controlled by both the law and the Gaming Board.

Gaming licences must be obtained – these are granted by local licensing magistrates on an annual basis. For both first applications and renewals, notices must be served with advertisements in the local press. Objections can be sent to the justices clerk and objectors have a right to be heard when the application is considered. Until recently, gaming licence applications were heard only in May of each year; now they can be heard at any time of the year. There are many grounds on which a gaming licence can be refused – particularly, the licensing justices must be satisfied there is substantial unsatisfied demand; the premises must be suitable; and noise, nuisance, lack of parking facilities or inadequate fire precautions are all reasons which might be used to reject an application. If a licence is granted, conditions or restrictions can be imposed.

Obtaining a licence is insufficient in itself – the *Gaming Board* has concurrent powers. So before application for a licence can be made, a certificate from the Gaming Board is required. Such certificates are given if the board approves. Though the board has to act fairly, it does not have to give reasons for refusing consent. The board will retain oversight of a casino which has been granted its certificate and licence through its full time inspectors (paid out of a levy on the casinos) who have wide powers of entry and inspection. The certificate can be withdrawn by the board but only on specified grounds, eg it finds it was given wrong information. If the board is dissatisfied on other grounds, it can object to renewal of the licence.

In general, the principle underlying these rules is that facilities should be sufficient to satisfy unstimulated demand for gaming – but no more. Various rules buttress this idea.

(a) *Permitted area*: Casinos cannot get a certificate or licence for a location outside a permitted area – largely big towns or holiday resorts.

(b) *The 48 hour rule*: Members of a casino can only take part in gaming if they were admitted to membership more than 48 hours previously after personal application. The idea is to prevent entry on an impulse – personal application and a two-day wait are needed. *Bona fide* guests of existing members are however allowed to participate.

(c) *Live entertainment* in the form of musicians, cabaret or dancing is prohibited – as it might be an attraction to take part in gaming.

(d) *Advertisements* of a casino are prohibited except for a sign on the premises, a single notice in a newspaper to state a licence has been granted or advertisements in overseas newspapers. Artificial stimulation of demand is again prevented.

(c) *Hours of gaming* are limited but not ungenerous. Play on Sunday is allowed, but hours are limited to afternoons and evenings through to the early hours (up to 4 am most nights)

(f) *No credit rule*: It is an offence for a casino operator (or his staff) to allow any credit for gaming, whether by funding in advance or allowing credit in order to gamble or to cover losses. The idea is to prevent a gambler playing beyond his means on easy credit. (Of course, anyone else can advance credit.) The only exception to this 'chips for cash' rule is that a player's cheque will be accepted; but it cannot be backdated and must be presented within two days. If the gambler's cheque 'bounces' (ie it is dishonoured by his bank) the casino can sue for the sum due because 'gaming' is not a wagering contract. A successful player can likewise sue for winnings due.

The *games* played in a casino are of two types and regulations exist under the statute law to regulate each.

(A) Conventional banker's games are games of unequal chance of which roulette is the most popular, but also include blackjack, baccarat banque, punto banco and chemin de fer. In each case, the existence of the bank gives the casino its edge and secures its profit. The regulations ensure that the gambler is not 'taken for a ride'. They forbid, for example, two zeros on roulette wheels or the more extreme 'mug options' at blackjack.

(B) Card-room games are games of equal chance such as backgammon, poker and dice. Here the casino takes its profit in the form of a commission on winnings or a participation fee. It is cheaper, of course, to play in private.

(iii) Gaming in Proprietary Clubs

Where genuine members' club, miners' welfare institutes and the like wish to provide gaming facilities as a purely incidental activity, without a profit motive but perhaps benefiting club funds in a minor way, the law allows a registration procedure to make such activities lawful.

Such a members' club does not require a certificate from the Gaming Board, but registration is by the local gaming licensing justices and the procedure is similar to that for a full casino licence. The club must satisfy the justices that it is a permanent members' club with over 25 members and that the principal purpose for which the club is established is not gaming. Registration procedure therefore is quite elaborate but once achieved the club can make charges for gaming sufficient for a modest profit to benefit general funds. Regulations allow the nonbanker games and some of the banker games such as pontoon and chemin de fer. Few clubs now bother to register and content themselves with gaming machines and bingo.

72

(iv) Gaming Machines

A gaming machine is constructed for playing a game of chance, with a slot for the insertion of coins or tokens. This wide definition not only includes fruit machines but also 'amusement only' machines where the player can (at best) hope for his money back.

Three main types of machine exist – each with different rules.

(A) 'Jackpot machines': These offer large cash prizes and are usually of the fruit machine variety. To operate these, premises are required with either (a) a casino licence, or (b) a bingo club licence, or (c) being a members' club, registration with the licensing authority.

In all cases: no more than two machines are allowed; a single play must not exceed a statutory figure, recently increased to 20 pence; prizes must be in cash, not tokens. There is no limit on the amount of the jackpot, but giving the prize in cash by the machine imposes some practical limit and is rarely more than £100.

(B) 'Amusement with prizes' machines: These machines, sometimes of the fruit machine variety, can be installed in public places which have a permit – granted by the local authority or, in the case of a pub, by the licensing justices. The authority can limit the number of machines. These machines are widely found, in pubs, cafés, arcades and shops. For such machines: the maximum charge for play must not exceed 10 pence; the maximum cash prize is fixed by law – currently it is £ 1.50, but a nonmonetary prize can be of a value of up to £3; if the prize is in the form of tokens a player must be able to exchange his tokens for goods or noncash prizes. Travelling showmen and travelling fairground operators do not require a permit.

(C) Games without prizes: if no prize is offered a permit is not required. These machines are usually found in fairground and amusement arcades.

The only exception to the above rules are for persons or organisations holding bazaars, fêtes, sporting meets or indeed any charity or other non-commercial entertainments. If (and only if) gaming is incidental to the main purpose, gaming machines (including jackpot machines) can be provided, but none of the proceeds can be taken for private gain.

(v) Bingo

Bingo is a lottery played as a game and whenever it is played for money stakes it is a form of gaming, but specific rules apply to relax the full rigour of the law. Bingo can lawfully be played: (i) in licensed clubs, (ii) in members' club.

(A) Commercial Clubs (1,270 clubs were licensed in 1985) dominate organised bingo and operators who have a magistrates' licence limited to bingo operate under relaxed rules:

(1) To participate a person only has to apply for membership 24 hours in advance – and usually a very nominal fee payable.

(2) Licences are available in all parts of the country.

(3) Shows and entertainment, forbidden in gaming establishments, are allowed. This allows provision of up to two gaming machines.

(4) Limited 'Linked' Bingo is allowed, providing for simultaneous games on more than one premises, but with a weekly prize limit of £3,000. The Gaming (Bingo) Act 1985, which came into force on 9 June 1986, allows multiple bingo by licensed bingo clubs for maximum prizes of £50,000.

(5) The proprietors can enhance the prizes by up to £1,250, but otherwise they must not exceed the total amount staked.

In bingo, unlike the football pools, the total stake is redistributed as winnings. The promoter make his profit from the entrance fee (about 20-25p a session) and a participation fee for each game or series of games. There is then an enforceable legal contract between the player and promoter, and either can sue in a dispute. The only sum deducted from the stakes is bingo duty.

Despite these relaxations, operators require the usual certificate from the Gaming Board and a magistrates' licence, which requires annual renewal.

(B) Prize bingo, where the winnings are not in money but goods, is not gaming but an amusement with prizes and is therefore found on fairgrounds and the like, with a local authority permit. It is also used in commercial bingo clubs, who require no extra permit to play this game, often during the 'interval'; the promoter can take a cut of the stakes. Stakes are limited to 10 pence.

(vi) Bridge and Whist Clubs

Bridge and whist, despite the degree of skill that is involved, involve an element of equal chance and are covered by gaming legislation – though as 'non-banker' games, they can be played without licence or registration provided the limits on permissible entry charges are observed. Special provision has been made here and bridge and whist clubs can charge £6 per person per day compared to 15 pence for all other games.

5. Lotteries

A lottery is a distribution of prizes by lot or pure chance. No skill is involved; if there is a degree of skill, it is not a lottery.

Lotteries are illegal unless they come within one the exceptions set out below. All lotteries for private gain are unlawful. It may appear paradoxical that lotteries (which appear relatively harmless compared to other forms of gambling) are strictly controlled: the reason is that they present the greatest possibility for fraud: the punter does not see what is happening to his money. There is also the risk of inducing people to spend more than they can afford.

The following lotteries, in 'ascending' order of scope, are lawful. A promoter of a lottery must ensure that the types are not mixed:

(i) Small Lotteries
These are lotteries incidental to entertainments and activities such as bazaars, fêtes, dinners, sales of work or sporting events (and those of similar character); they are lawful, whether they are for a single day, or longer, provided:
(a) The lottery is not the main purpose or inducement of the event
(b) Tickets are sold only at the event
(c) No more than £50 can be taken from the proceeds for prizes
(d) Cash prizes are prohibited
(e) All proceeds, after deduction of expenses and up to £50 for prizes, must be devoted to purposes other than private gain.
(f) The result must be declared during the event. Small lotteries require no registration or special tickets and are common.

(ii) Private Lotteries
Private lotteries are those organised exclusively among a group of people who either work together, are all members of one society or club (but *not* a gaming club) or who are all resident on the same premises (eg, students in a hall of residence).

Again, no registration is required, but stricter rules must be kept.

(a) Printing expenses can be deducted; otherwise the whole proceeds must go on prizes, or if a club or society, part on prizes and part to the purposes of the society.
(b) No advertisements of the lottery are allowed – except a notice on the premises.
(c) The price of every ticket must be the same – and stated on the ticket.
(d) Each ticket must include on its face the name and address of the persons to whom sale is restricted and a statement that prizes can only be delivered to the person to whom the ticket was sold.
(e) Cash or value must be paid for each ticket.
(f) Tickets cannot go on general sale or be sent through the post.

Though no registration is required, private lotteries do need specially printed or prepared tickets.

(iii) Public Lotteries
Public lotteries are also known as *Society lotteries* and are the ones perhaps most frequently encountered. Registration (on payment of a fee, currently £25) with the local authority is required; once so registered a charitable sporting, cultural or other society not established for commercial activity can conduct up to 52 lotteries in any one year with a seven-day minimum

gap between each. Registration can only be refused on the grounds that one of the organisers has been convicted of fraud or a lotteries offence or that the club or society is not run on non-profit lines. The rules for society lotteries are detailed and must be strictly observed. Persons organising such lotteries must take care that they understand them and observe them. They are, in outline, as follows.

(1) The promoter must be a member of the society and authorised by the society to act on their behalf.
(2) Tickets must not exceed a specified sum, currently 50p; their total value must be limited; the present maximum is £10,000.
(3) Tickets must not be sold to a person under the age of 16.
(4) Tickets must not be sent through the post except to society members.
(5) Tickets must show the price, the name and address of the organisers and the date of the draw.
(6) Expenses must not exceed whichever is the lesser of (i) the actual expenses; (ii) 25% of the lottery proceeds (15% if the total proceeds exceed £10,000).
(7) There are limits as to the size of individual prizes; lotteries registered with the Gaming Board can give higher prizes but the current basic limit is £2,000. Total prizes must not exceed half the whole proceeds.
(8) The total amount raised after deduction of expenses and provision of prizes must be applied for the purposes of the society.
(9) The lottery cannot be advertised except to members or by a notice on the society premises.
(10) A return must be made to the local authority showing details of money raised, expenses deducted and the way the money raised is to be spent. Lotteries registered with the Gaming Board are allowed higher limits on both the maximum value of tickets sold and the maximum value of the prizes.

Breach of these rules is a criminal offence with maximum penalties of either a £400 fine or up to two years imprisonment.

(iv) Local Authority Lotteries
Local Councils are now permitted to raise money from lotteries, but must register with the Gaming Board. There are restrictions similar to those imposed on society lotteries, eg a maximum of 52 in any one year. The purpose and object of the lottery must be publicised and proceeds can only be applied for that object. Tickets can be sold publicly, through shops, kiosks or other outlets.

All other lotteries, except for a quaint 1846 exemption given to art unions, are illegal. No national lottery is now allowed, though many were held in earlier centuries, particularly in the eighteenth century. The last was in 1826. Many are held in other countries; and the 1978 Royal

Commission recommended a United Kingdom National Lottery for good causes: to date, this recommendation has not been acted upon.

6. Taxation on Gambling

Once the gambling activities described above became accepted, it was natural that they should be taxed. The principal taxes and duties are:

(A) General betting duty on bets with a bookmaker or on the Tote at horseraces or racing tracks. The duty is currently levied at 4% for on course betting and 8% off course.

(B) Pool betting duty is charged on all bets by way of pool betting, particularly on football pools. The amount of that duty is now a staggering 42½%. Thus, for every £1 you stake on the pools, 42½p is paid to the Exchequer.

(C) Gaming Machine licence duty is paid when licences for machines are given. The rates vary according to both the type of machine ('small prize' machines pay less) and to the number of machines authorised. The lowest duty levied is £120 per annum per machine; the highest £750.

(D) Gaming licence duty is a licence duty of £250 is payable on application. Further duties are payable on the gross gaming yield, beginning at a rate of 2½% and rising in stages to 33%; the greater the profit, the higher the duty.

(E) Bingo duty is charged at 10% of the money taken per week as charged for cards, plus one ninth of the net profit thereafter. Domestic or small scale play of bingo is exempt from duty.

(F) Income tax. In addition to the above duties, all profits from gambling activities are subject to income tax – even if they arise from illegal betting or gaming! Winnings to punters, however, are exempt from capital gains tax; and income tax will not be charged unless the punter is so successful that he makes his living from gambling.

Holidays

Holidays can give rise to a number of legal difficulties. We will first look at the legal implications of travelling by train, coach, and air. After that, passport and foreign travel will be examined, and then problems with travel agents and tour operators. Finally, we will look at related questions concerning hotels, restaurants and public houses.

1. Travelling by Train

When a passenger buys a ticket he makes a contract with British Rail (or with whoever operates the railway). That contract will be subject to standard conditions; in the case of British Rail, these are published in their booklet 'Conditions of Carriage of Passengers and their Luggage'. Below are some of the matters that are dealt with in the Conditions.

(i) Unavailability of Seats
Buying a ticket does not entitle a passenger to a seat and a second class passenger has no right to sit in first class when all second class seats are taken, unless invited by the guard or on payment of the difference between the first and second class fare. If a seat has been reserved, the conditions state that the reservation fee is refundable if no seat is available, but that no additional compensation will be payable. It is likely that a Court would consider this to be unreasonable and therefore not allow British Rail to rely on it.

(ii) Timetables and Train Services
Trains are not guaranteed to start or arrive on time, or indeed to run at all, and liability for any loss which a passenger may suffer as a result is excluded. It is possible that a Court would consider this provision to be unreasonable, and therefore order compensation to be paid where loss is suffered.

(iii) Loss of, or Damage to, Luggage
British Rail are not liable for loss of or damage to a passenger's luggage

unless it can be proved that the loss or damage resulted from British Rail's negligence. If, however, the luggage is carried in the guard's van, the onus is on British Rail to show that the loss or damage was not caused by their negligence. Liability is limited to £500 per passenger; whether this limit applies will depend on whether the Court considers it to be reasonable. It should be noted that the conditions do not, and cannot, exclude liability for death or personal injury caused by British Rail's negligence.

(iv) Complaints

Complaints about rail travel should be addressed in the first instance to the area manager. If satisfaction is not obtained, the Area Transport Users Consultative Committee should be approached.

2. Travelling by Coach

(i) Bookings

A passenger who has booked a seat on a coach has a contract with the operator. That contract will be breached if no seat is available, thereby preventing the passenger from travelling or forcing him to travel on a later coach or by different means. In these circumstances the passenger will be entitled to compensation for such expense as he might have been put to, for example, the additional cost of travelling by rail or the price of overnight accommodation. If the booking conditions contain a provision excluding or limited the operator's liability, the conditions must have been sufficiently drawn to the passenger's attention, and the provision must be reasonable if it is to be effective.

(ii) Delays

If a coach is seriously delayed, and this is the fault of the operator (for example, the coach breaks down because it has been inadequately maintained), it may be possible for a passenger to claim compensation. Booking conditions excluding liability for delay will only be effective if the Court considers them to be reasonable.

(iii) Accidents

If a coach is involved in an accident and this is a result of the driver's negligence or results from inadequate maintenance, a passenger can recover compensation from the operator for any physical injuries or damage to his property that may have been caused. Liability for personal injury cannot be excluded in the booking conditions and a clause excluding liability for property damage must be reasonable. If the accident is caused by another road user, it will be possible to sue that person if he was negligent.

(iv) Complaints

As well as seeking legal redress in appropriate circumstances, a complaint can be made to the Traffic Commissioners for the relevant area about dangerous or inadequate service. The Commissioners will investigate the matter and in extreme cases can revoke a coach operator's licence.

3. Travelling by Air

(i) Terms of Travel

The terms on which a flight between two or more countries is made are governed by an international agreement called the Warsaw Convention. This regulates the conditions which can be contained in the contract between the carrier and the passenger. These condition will be referred to in the ticket issued to the passenger.

(ii) Personal Injury

The carrier will be liable for the death of a passenger or personal injury which occurs on board the aircraft or in the process of getting on or off the aircraft. The carrier will not be liable if it can show that it took all the necessary measures to avoid the injury or that it was impossible to take such measures, unless the flight involves a stop in the United States, in which case this defence will not be available to the carrier. Where the carrier is liable, the Warsaw Convention limits the amount of compensation payable; the maximum amount in most cases at the moment is about £7,000, which means that it is sensible for a person travelling by air to take out appropriate insurance.

(iii) Loss of, and Damage to, Baggage

The carrier will be liable for lost or damaged luggage, unless it can show that all necessary measures were taken to avoid the loss or damage. Liability is limited, however, to about £12 per kilo unless the value of the baggage is declared in advance and the appropriate supplementary charge paid. It is important to report any loss or damage immediately as very short time-limits are imposed for claiming compensation.

(iv) Delay

A carrier is liable to pay compensation if passengers or baggage are delayed beyond what is reasonable, except where the delay is due to factors beyond the carrier's control. An airline might be required to compensate a passenger for an overnight stay at a hotel, for instance, where the unavailability of a plane has made this necessary. Damages might also be payable for causing a passenger to lose part of his holiday.

(v) Overbooking
If the plane has been overbooked and a passenger is denied a seat, the airline will be liable to the passenger for breach of contract. Many airlines now operate a scheme whereby they offer compensation in accordance with a fixed scale in the event of overbooking. It will usually be advisable to accept the compensation offered unless the passenger's loss is significantly greater, rather than take legal action against the airline.

(vi) Complaints
The Air Transport User's Committee will investigate complaints made by passengers about problems arising out of air travel, for example, with respect to lost luggage or overbooking. The committee will give advice but cannot award compensation.

4. Passports and Travelling Abroad

(i) Types of Passport
It is necessary to have a passport in order to enter another country. There are two types of British passport – the standard passport and the visitor's passport. The standard passport is valid for use in all countries and lasts for ten years. The visitor's passport may be used in most West European countries and in a number of countries outside Europe, including Canada. It is only valid for one year. The holder's husband or wife and children under sixteen can be included on either type of passport, but they can only travel with the passport holder. If they wish to travel alone they must obtain a separate passport. Children over five are entitled to a passport in their own name, for which parents or guardians must apply.

(ii) How to obtain a passport
Application forms for either type of passport are available at Post Offices. A visitor's passport can be issued at the Post Office, but it will be necessary to have the application form signed first by a minister of religion, doctor, teacher or person of similar standing. The current fee is £7.50, or £11.25 if the husband/wife of the holder is to be included. In the case of a standard passport, the completed application form must be sent to the appropriate regional passport office, together with the fee of £15, or £22.50 where the husband/wife of the holder is included. The application should be sent at least four weeks before the planned journey. It may be sensible for someone who travels abroad frequently to apply for a passport which contains 94 pages for visas and entry stamps, rather than the usual 30. These cost twice as much as the 30 page passport, but when the latter is a full a new passport, at the full fee, must be obtained.

(iii) Visas

Some countries will only allow admission to persons to whom a visa has been issued. Travel agents or the consulate of the country to be visited will give information about this.

(iv) Health Care Abroad

Visitors from the United Kingdom are entitled to receive immediate necessary medical treatment in countries which are members of the EEC. In most cases, however, it is necessary to obtain a Form E111 from the Department of Health and Social Security before travelling. The UK has reciprocal health arrangements with a number of other countries, in which emergency treatment can be obtained free or at reduced rates. Information about these can be obtained from the leaflet SA 30, obtainable from the DHSS. In countries with which there are no health agreements, persons needing treatment will have to pay the full cost, which means that adequate health and accident insurance cover is desirable if these countries are to be visited.

(v) Criminal Offences Abroad

A visitor to a foreign country will be subject to the local law, which may well be different from English law. If an offence is committed, it is no excuse that the offender did not know that what he was doing was illegal. If a traveller is arrested he should ask the police to contact the British Consulate immediately.

5. Problems with Travel Agents and Tour Operators

A number of problems can arise with holidays booked through travel agents. The travel agent might go bankrupt before the holiday takes place, the trip might be cancelled, a different date or hotel might be substituted at the last minute, or the hotel facilities might be very disappointing. If these things occur the holiday-maker may be entitled to compensation. In the case of a package holiday, the contract will usually be with a tour operator rather than with the agent through whom the holiday-maker books, and so generally it is the tour operator who should be pursued if things go wrong.

(i) Booking Conditions

Many travel agents and tour operators are members of the Association of British Travel Agents (ABTA). Brochures and booking conditions used by members must comply with the minimum standards laid down by ABTA. These help to ensure that the conditions are fair and clearly set out the respective rights and obligations of the holiday-maker and the provider of the holiday. For example, booking conditions may not give the operator the right to cancel a holiday after the date on which payment of the balance of the price of the holiday becomes due, except when forced to do so by hostilities, political unrest or other such circumstances beyond the operator's control. Where an operator does cancel a holiday, he is required by the ABTA rules to offer the holiday-maker a choice of a comparable holiday or a full refund. It may be noted that if an operator cancels a holiday otherwise than as a result of factors which are beyond his control, the holiday-maker has a right under the general law to compensation, but acceptance of a comparable holiday will often be a more appropriate solution.

Booking conditions are also likely to contain provisions relating to variations in the holiday booked and surcharges. The ABTA rules require prompt notification of alterations and insist that if a major alteration is made (for example, delayed departure or change in hotel), the holiday-maker shall be given the option either to cancel the holiday and receive a full refund, or to accept the new arrangements which must be of at least a comparable standard. Booking conditions which purport to give the tour operator the right to change the holiday details without paying compensation or giving the holiday-maker the option to cancel are likely to be legally ineffective. A tour operator can only make a surcharge (that is, increase the cost of the holiday beyond the price at which it was booked) if the booking conditions allow this. Provisions are often included which permit the price of a holiday to be increased as a result of currency movements or other increases in costs which are beyond the tour operator's control.

(ii) Cancellation by the Holiday-maker
Once a firm booking has been made, the holiday-maker does not in normal circumstances have the right to cancel the holiday. If he does, the tour operator will usually be allowed to retain the whole of the deposit which the holiday-maker has paid. Since cancellation will constitute a breach of contract, the tour operator will also be entitled to damages for his loss of profit if he is not able to sell the holiday to someone else. Booking conditions often specify that a certain percentage of the cost of the holiday may be retained by the operator, in excess of the deposit. The nearer the cancellation of the holiday to the date that it is due to take place, the higher the percentage will be. If booking conditions provide for a large retention even where ample notice of cancellation is given, someone cancelling a holiday should consider challenging this.

(iii) Disappointing Holidays
The facilities promised in the brochure should be available during the holiday, and the accommodation and service should be of a standard commensurate with the price paid. The case of Jarvis v Swans Tours Ltd on page 84

Jarvis v Swans Tours Ltd

In *Jarvis v Swans Tours Ltd,* decided in 1972, Mr Jarvis booked a 'houseparty' holiday for two weeks in Switzerland with Swans Tours. Mr Jarvis was to take the holiday on his own, and the brochure promised the following arrangements: 'Welcome party on arrival. Afternoon tea and cake . . . Swiss Dinner by candlelight. *Fondue* party. Yodler evening . . . farewell party.' The brochure also said that the resident host spoke English, that there were ski runs nearby and that skis would be available. The total cost of the holiday was just over £63. The holiday turned out to be very disappointing. In the first week the houseparty consisted of only thirteen people. During the second week Mr Jarvis was the only person staying, and as the host did not speak English, he had no one to talk to. There was no welcome party; the cake for tea consisted of potato crisps and dry nut-cake and the yodler evening was no more than a local man in his working clothes who sang four or five songs very quickly. The ski-runs were some distance away and in the first week there were only mini-skis available. These rubbed Mar Jarvis's feet which meant that he could not ski at all in the second week. When he got home Mr Jarvis sued Swans tours and he was awarded £125 damages. Mr Jarvis was entitled to have the benefit of the features mentioned in the brochure and the Court could order a tour operator to pay in damages a sum greater than the cost of the holiday. People go on holiday to enjoy themselves and where a holiday is ruined because of the absence of the advertised facilities the damages should reflect this fact.

illustrates in what circumstances a tour operator will be liable to pay compensation when a holiday does not live up to the expectations that the brochure creates.

(iv) Conciliation and Arbitration Scheme

If something goes wrong on a holiday booked with an ABTA member, ABTA offer a conciliation service and an arbitration scheme. As regards the former, a conciliator studies the complaint made by the holiday-maker and any correspondence between him and the tour operator, and suggests terms on which the dispute might be settled. The tour operator cannot, however, be compelled to accept the terms put forward. If a complaint about a package tour cannot be satisfactorily resolved, the holiday-maker may make use of the arbitration scheme which is operated on behalf of ABTA by the Chartered Institute of Arbitrators. An application, on the prescribed form, must normally be made within 9 months of returning from the holiday, and can be made by anyone mentioned in the booking form. The scheme does not apply where a claim is made for more than £1,000 per person or £5,000 per booking form, or where the claim in very complicated or largely in respect of physical injury or illness. Disputes are decided purely on the basis of written submissions – there is no oral hearing. A fee of £17.25 for a single claimant (there is a small additional charge for further claimants) is made for this service. The decision of the arbitrator will be binding on both the holiday-maker and the tour operator. Instead of using the arbitration scheme, or where the tour operator is not an ABTA member, a holiday-maker can seek redress in the Courts. This will involve a more formal procedure and may be more expensive.

(v) Bankruptcy of Travel Agent or Tour Operator

ABTA members are required to provide financial bonds or guarantees. This means that monies paid to a travel agent or tour operator in advance of a holiday will be reimbursed if they become insolvent. ABTA also has an insurance indemnity scheme in respect of insolvent travel agents. In certain cases, there is protection even where a tour operator is not an ABTA member. Operators who are required to take out an Air Travel Organisers Licence, for instance, must give a financial bond, as must members of certain other travel organisations, for example, the Bus and Coach Council.

(vi) Holiday Insurance

Given the various things that can go wrong with a holiday, insurance cover is undoubtedly an extremely sensible precaution. Some tour operators insist that their own policy is used; where this is so the policy should be carefully checked to make sure that it is adequate. The following risks should be covered:

(a) Cancellation. This should provide for reimbursement of all amounts payable in respect of the holiday which are not recoverable from the tour operator, if the holiday has to be cancelled by the holiday-maker as a result of some unforeseen event;

(b) Delay. Compensation for delay will not be payable by the tour operator if this is caused by adverse weather conditions or strikes, and hence insurance cover is advisable to pay for an overnight stay at a hotel or similar expenses which stem from the delay;

(c) Medical expenses. The amount of cover required depends on the country to be visited. For member countries of the European Economic Community it should be at least £25,000. For the United States a minimum of £500,000 would be appropriate.

(d) Accident. Death and personal injury should be covered, including the cost of the journey home, where appropriate; personal liability covers damages that may have to be paid by the insured person as a result of causing injury or property damage to a third person.

(e) Luggage and personal property. The policy should cover the full replacement value of all property taken on holiday; most policies limit the amount payable in respect of an individual item and in respect of money carried abroad.

6. Hotels

(i) The Duty to Supply Food and Accommodation

If an establishment is a 'hotel' as defined by the Hotel Proprietors Act 1956, the owner is under a duty to provide accommodation and supply food and drink to all travellers unless he has a reasonable ground for refusal. Premises will be a hotel within the definition in the Act where the proprietor holds the premises out as offering food and accommodation on these terms. Where the proprietor does not represent that he is willing to take all-comers, therefore, the establishment will not fall within the provisions of the Act. This will be so, for instance, in the case of a 'private hotel' or 'residential hotel', or private house offering bed and breakfast. A public house may often include the word 'hotel' within its name, but if no accommodation is provided, it will not be within the Act either.

As well as being under a duty to accommodate a traveller, a hotel-keeper must also store his luggage, and, if he has space, the traveller's car. A hotel-keeper is even obliged to take in a guest's dog, unless, as observed in *R v Rymer* in 1877, the dog is dangerous or unclean! The proprietor is discharged from his obligation to provide accommodation if the hotel is full, and, if food and drink have run out, he is not liable for failing to provide it. Facilities may be denied to travellers who are drunk or are otherwise in an objectionable state. The proprietor may also demand payment of a reasonable sum in advance, and if this is not forthcoming, or the traveller otherwise appears unable to pay, he may refuse accommodation. A hotel keeper who wrongfully denies facilities to a traveller is liable to prosecution, and the traveller may sue him for damages.

If premises are not a hotel within the meaning of the Act, the proprietor may, subject to what follows, deny accommodation or refreshment to a person who requests it without giving any reason. The landlord of a public house, for instance, may, at his discretion, refuse to serve a customer. Even where the premises are not a hotel, however, but are a boarding house or similar establishment, it is an offence to refuse to provide accommodation, or to refuse to provide accommodation of similar quality and on similar terms to those normally offered by the proprietor to the public at large, on grounds of colour, race, nationality, ethnic or national origin (Race Relations Act 1976) or on grounds of sex (Sex Discrimination Act 1975). Where a traveller has booked a room in any type of accommodation but, when the time comes, there is no room available, the proprietor will be in breach of contract and will be liable to compensate the traveller for any losses he may have suffered. This might include the additional cost of staying in a more expensive hotel, for example.

(ii) Display of Prices

All hotels, as defined above, which have four or more rooms or eight or more beds must display a notice setting out information about the prices of rooms. The notice must be placed in a prominent position in the reception area, or if there isn't one, at the entrance, where it can be easily read by anyone seeking sleeping accommodation at the hotel. The notice must state the current price (including any service charge payable) per night of:

(1) a bedroom for occupation by one adult;
(2) a bedroom for occupation by two adults;
(3) a bed other than one situated in a room for one or two persons; in this case it must be stated whether the bed is in a dormitory or a room to be shared with other guests.

Where rooms within a category have different prices, it is sufficient to state the highest and lowest prices within the category.

The notice must also state whether the prices include value added tax; if they do not, the amount of tax payable must be expressed as a monetary amount. If the room charge includes meals, which meals are being paid for must be indicated.

A hotel which does not display the above information will be liable to prosecution under the Tourism (Sleeping Accommodation Price Display) Order 1977. A guest who is dissatisfied should complain to the local trading standards department.

(iii) *Responsibility for Guest's Safety*

Anyone providing accommodation, whether it technically constitutes a hotel or not, must take reasonable care to see that guests are not injured as a result of the condition of the premises. Where a passage is insufficiently lit, for example, and it ought to be anticipated that guests will use it at night, the proprietor will be liable to pay damages to a guest who is injured. The proprietor cannot exclude his liability for causing death or personal injury as a result of his negligence by putting up a notice, since the Unfair Contract Terms Act 1977 makes such provisions ineffective.

(iv) *Responsibility for Guest's Property*

The proprietor of a hotel, as defined above, will generally be liable to a guest whose property is lost, stolen or damaged. Subject to what will be said below, the hotel-keeper's liability is strict, which means that he is liable even though the loss or damage is not a result of his negligence or that of his employees. This rule applies where the property was situated within the hotel buildings at the time of the loss or damage, or in a place so closely connected with the buildings as to be treated as part of them. For liability to be strict, it is not necessary for the hotel-keeper to take the goods into his custody for safekeeping. The hotel-keeper is not liable, however, for loss or damage to vehicles, or property contained in them, unless it can be proved that he or his employees were negligent.

The hotel-keeper's liability will only be strict, as opposed to depending on proof of negligence, where: (1) at the time of the loss or damage sleeping accommodation at the hotel had been engaged for the traveller who owned the property in question and (2) the loss or damage occurred during the period commencing with midnight immediately preceding, and ending with the midnight immediately following, a period for which the traveller was a guest at the hotel and entitled to use the accommodation so engaged.

The hotel keeper will not be strictly liable if the loss or damage results from the negligence of the guest himself. It may amount to negligence for a guest to leave his door unlocked, but this is not necessarily so and will depend on the particular circumstances of the case.

A hotel-keeper can limit the amount of his strict liability by displaying a notice in the form prescribed by the Hotel Proprietors Act 1956. The notice is shown below.

NOTICE
Loss of or Damage to Guests' Property
Under the Hotel Proprietors Act 1956, an hotel proprietor may in certain circumstances be liable to make good any loss of or damage to a guest's property even though it was not due to any fault of the proprietor or staff of the hotel.
This liability however–

(a) extends only to the property of guests who have engaged sleeping accommodation at the hotel;
(b) is limited to £50 for any one article and a total of £100 in the case of any one guest, except in the case of property that has been deposited, or offered for deposit, for safe custody;
(c) does not cover motor-cars or other vehicles of any kind or any property left in them, or horses or other live animals.

This notice does not constitute an admission either that the Act applies to this hotel or that liability thereunder attaches to the proprietor of this hotel in any particular case.

In order to be effective, the notice, printed in plain type, must have been conspicuously displayed in a place where it could conveniently be read by guests at or near the reception office or desk, or where there is no such office or desk, at or near the main entrance. Assuming that these requirements are satisfied, the notice will be effective in accordance with its terms, that is, the hotel will not be liable for more than £50 per article, and a total of £100 to any one guest. If the notice is misprinted, however, it will not operate at all.

Where a notice of the kind set out above is properly displayed, the hotel will still be liable if the guest's property was lost or stolen as a result of the negligence of the proprietor or of his employees. In the case of an establishment providing accommodation which is not a 'hotel' for the purpose of the Act, negligence will be the only basis for the proprietor's liability. Liability for negligence which causes loss or damage to property can only be avoided by the proprietor if there is an effective exclusion clause in the contract between himself and the guest. This involves three things: the exclusion clause must be a part of the contract entered into when it is agreed that the guest shall be allowed to stay; its wording must exclude liability for what has happened, and the clause must be a reasonable one. If the latter requirement is not satisfied the clause will be made ineffective by the Unfair Contract Terms Act 1977. The reasonableness requirement will generally be difficult to satisfy. The case of *Olley v Marlborough Court Ltd* (page 90), decided in 1948, illustrates when an exclusion clause will be treated as being part of a contract for accommodation in a hotel.

(v) Hotel's Right to Detain Guests' Property
If a guest is unable to pay the bill when he leaves, the hotel is entitled to detain the guest's luggage or other property brought into the hotel (not a guest's car) as security for payment. The proprietor may ultimately sell the property if the bill is not paid.

7. Restaurants

(i) Bookings
A firm booking of a table constitutes a contract between the customer and the restaurant and so if a table is not available within a reasonable time after the time for which it is booked the restaurant will be in breach of contract. The customer will be entitled to damages if he can show that he has suffered a loss – for example, the cost of travelling to and from the restaurant or to an alternative restaurant. By the same token, if the customer does not turn up the restaurant will be able to sue him for any profit they may have lost. It will probably be otherwise, however, if plenty of notice of cancellation is given; the restaurant may then be able to use the table for another customer and so will not suffer a loss of profit.

(ii) Prices
By regulations made under the Prices Act 1974, a restaurant must display a menu and wine list with prices at or near the entrance of the eating area, which will normally mean outside or just inside the door. In a self-service restaurant, prices must be visible at the place where food is chosen. If the restaurant serves more than 30 different items, the prices of only 30 items need be quoted. Where the restaurant is licensed, the prices of at least six different wines must be given, or if fewer than six are offered, of all of

them. The price list must be in an obvious position and be easy to read. The prices quoted must include value added tax. If there is a service charge, or a minimum charge, information concerning these must be displayed at least as prominently as the price of the food.

If this information is not displayed the restaurant will be committing a criminal offence. Also, if it has not been made reasonably clear before the meal is ordered that there is a service charge, or that the meal is subject to a minimum charge, the customer is entitled to refuse to pay it.

(iii) Quantity of Food and Drink
The law does not lay down minimum quantities of food to be served, but if quantities or weights of food are indicated in the menu, these must be complied with. If wine is sold in a carafe, the amount contained must be indicated.

(iv) Quality of Food
The rules about hygiene in restaurants, and in premises selling food generally, are strict. These are contained in the Food Act 1984 and the

---

Olley v Marlborough Court Ltd

Mr and Mrs Olley were guests in the defendant's private residential hotel. (It was not a 'hotel' for the purposes of what is now the Hotel Proprietors Act 1956 and hence the proprietor would only be liable for loss or damage to guests' property if negligent.) The contract to stay at the hotel was entered into at the reception desk when the Olleys first arrived – the proprietor agreed to let them stay in return for payment in accordance with the hotel's usual rates. The Olleys then went up to their room; there was a notice on the bedroom wall to the following effect:

'The proprietors will not hold themselves responsible for articles lost or stolen, unless handed to the manageress for safe custody. Valuables should be deposited for safe custody in a sealed package and a receipt obtained.'

Sometime later Mrs Olley went out and placed her room key, as requested, on a board in the reception office. During her absence an unknown person removed the key from the board, entered her room and stole a fur coat and other valuable property. It was held that the hotel had been negligent. They had not taken reasonable care to ensure that unauthorised persons did not take the key and thereby gain access to the Olleys' room. It was also held by the Court that the hotel could not rely on the exclusion notice on the wall of the Olley's bedroom because it was not a part of the contract – this had been formed at the reception desk and any notice that could only be seen subsequently came too late to be incorporated into the contract.

regulations made under it. Premises must be clean and sanitary, and there must be adequate lavatory and washing facilities for staff, for example. Non-compliance with the regulations is a criminal offence and the Court can make a compensation order in favour of a customer who has suffered as a result of poor hygiene standards. The Court can also close down an unhygienic restaurant. If a customer thinks that a restaurant's standards of hygiene are unsatisfactory, a complaint should be made to the local environmental health officer.

Food and drink must be fit for human consumption. The sale of items which do not satisfy this requirement is a criminal offence even if the restaurant did not know that the food was defective and even though there has been no negligence. It is also an offence to sell food and drink which is not of the nature, substance and quality demanded. If bread is stated on the menu as being baked with wholemeal flour, for instance, this must be the case. As well as imposing a criminal penalty for breach of these requirements, the Court can also award compensation to the customer. An extreme illustrate of selling 'food' which was not fit for human consumption, and which was not of the nature demanded, is *Meah v Roberts*, decided in 1977 (see below).

Meah v Roberts

In this case, a husband and wife took their two children to a restaurant and ordered lemonade for them. A colourless liquid, resembling lemonade, was poured from a lemonade bottle and the children started to drink it. The bottle did not contain lemonade but a strong solution of caustic soda which was used for cleaning the pipes of the equipment from which lager was served. One of the children was seriously injured as a result. The caustic soda had been put in the bottle and left behind the bar by a brewery representative. He had explained to one of the waiters what the liquid was for, but the waiter did not speak much English and did not understand. Both the restaurant and the brewery, as employer of the representative, were prosecuted, and compensation was ordered to be paid to the children.

A customer can also bring civil proceedings in respect of food poisoning which results from food eaten in a restaurant. The person who pays for the meal can bring an action under the Sale of Goods Act 1979 and does not have to prove negligence on the part of the restaurant. Whether other members of a party can sue without proving negligence depends on whether they have a contract with the restaurant. In *Lockett v A & M Charles Ltd*, decided in 1938, a husband and wife had a meal in a restaurant and the wife subsequently became ill. There was no evidence as to who actually ordered the meal, but it was paid for by the husband. It was held by the Court that there was a contract between the restaurant and the wife: unless one member of the party is obviously 'in charge of proceedings' each customer is liable to the restaurant to pay for the meal and hence if the meal is defective each customer can sue the restaurant for breach of contract. Where the contract is only with one member of the party, a guest can only sue the restaurant if there has been negligence on its part. The restaurant would not be liable to the guest for instance, if it sold food which was infected when they received it, and there was no means of detecting that there was something wrong with it and all proper cooking and serving procedures had been followed.

If the food or drink served is not what was ordered, or is substandard, the customer is entitled to reject it. Where a meal is very poor, the customer might decide not to pay for it or to pay only such amount as he considers it was worth. If he does this, he should give his name and address to the proprietor. It is a criminal offence under the Thefts Acts 1968 and 1978 to leave a restaurant with a dishonest intention of avoiding payment. If the customer gives his name and address this will enable the restaurant proprietor to sue him if he wants to (he will fail if the meal was seriously substandard), but the matter will not be of interest to the police unless there is a risk that a breach of the peace might ensue!

(v) Damage to Customers' Property and Loss of Property
If a waiter spills food onto a customer, the restaurant will be liable to reimburse the customer the cost of having affected items of clothing cleaned, or the cost of a replacement if a garment is damaged beyond repair, providing the waiter was negligent. This will be so, for instance, where he was not paying proper attention to what he was doing. A restaurant is responsible for taking reasonable care of customers' property that is under its control. If a coat is handed in to a cloakroom attendant, or if the waiter takes it away, for example, the restaurant must take reasonable steps to make sure that it is safe from theft or damage. If a customer hangs his coat up in the eating area, however, it is his own responsibility to protect it. Where a restaurant has failed in its duty to safeguard a customer's property, but tries to rely on a notice excluding liability, the notice will only be effective if it is clear and sited in a prominent position, and if its terms are reasonable.

(iv) Alcoholic Drinks in Restaurants
A restaurant must be in possession of a licence if it serves alcoholic drinks and drinks may only be supplied to persons who are taking a meal. The restaurant will be bound by the local licensing hours (the same as those applying to public houses), though many restaurants will have a supper hour certificate, which allows them to serve alcohol up to 3pm in respect of the lunchtime session, and for an hour after the usual public house closing time in the evening.

8. Public Houses

(i) Right to be Served
There is no right to be served in a public house, though an offence is committed if the reason for refusal is the race or sex of the customer.

(ii) Who May Enter and Be Served in a Public House
The Licensing Act 1964 imposes restrictions on who may enter licensed premises, and on the consumption by and the sale of alcohol to young persons.

(1) An alcoholic drink may not be sold in the bar for consumption by a person under the age of eighteen. An offence is committed by the landlord if this restriction is knowingly breached. An offence is also committed by the young person if he buys or attempts to buy an alcoholic drink, or if he consumes alcohol in the bar, with the exception of certain drinks taken with meals (see (2) below). A person who buys or attempts to buy a drink for a person under eighteen for consumption in the bar can also be prosecuted.

(2) A person under eighteen but over sixteen can be served with beer, porter, cider or perry for consumption with a meal, in a part of the premises usually set aside for the service of meals which is not a bar.

(3) Persons under eighteen but over fourteen are allowed into a bar, but must not consume or buy alcohol. Children under fourteen are not permitted to go into the bar at all (except to pass through, eg to the toilet, where there is no other convenient route).

For the purpose of these rules, a 'bar' is defined as including 'any place exclusively or mainly used for the sale and consumption of intoxicating liquor'. This rather vague definition can give rise to problems in certain cases, but it is generally safe to assume that children under fourteen are allowed to be present in a pub garden or 'children's room', since these are unlikely to be classified as being part of the bar.

(iii) Opening Hours
Opening hours vary in different parts of the country. The general rule is that public houses can open from 11am to 11pm from Monday to Saturday, and from 12 noon to 3pm and 7pm to 10.30pm on Sundays, Christmas Day and Good Friday. Extensions can be obtained for special occasions and where meals are served or there is permitted music and dancing.

A customer is allowed ten minutes drinking-up time after closing time is called. Once that time has expired the drink must be left (it must not be taken from the premises) and no drinks may be served during drinking-up time. Drinking-up time is 30 minutes if the drink is served with a meal.

(iv) Quantities Sold

Alcoholic drinks may only be sold in public houses in recognised quantities. These are stipulated by the Weights and Measures Act 1963. Draught beer and cider can only be served in quantities of one-third of a pint, one half pint or multiples of a half-pint. The drink must be served in a glass which has its capacity marked on it or from an instrument which dispenses a measured quantity. Gin, rum, vodka and whisky can only be sold in quantities of one-quarter, one-fifth or one-sixth of a gill, or multiples of these. Wine sold for consumption on the premises must be sold in quantities of 25cl, 50cl, 1 litre, 10 fl oz or 20 fl oz, unless it is served in a closed bottle or by the glass. There are no stipulations as to how much a glass must contain. A notice must be displayed stating what measure is used for the spirits mentioned above and in what quantities wine is sold. A customer who thinks he has been given in short measure should complain to the local trading standards officer.

It is an offence for a public house to serve a larger measure – known as a 'long pull' – than was asked for, though few customers are inclined to complain! It is also illegal to supply drinks on credit in a public house.

(v) Display of Prices

The prices of drinks (and of any food being offered) must be displayed in a prominent position near where they are served. Where there are not more than 30 different items for sale, the price of each item must be given; where there are more than 30, the prices of at least 30 must be quoted. The price given must be for a drink of a stated measure.

(vi) Drunkenness

It is an offence under the Licensing Act 1964 for a licensee to permit drunkenness or 'violent, quarrelsome or riotous conduct' on licensed premises. A person who is drunk or is engaging in conduct of this kind can be prosecuted for refusing a request of the licensee for him to leave the premises. It is an offence to sell liquor to a drunken person. If the companions of someone who is drunk 'procure or attempt to procure' liquor for him, they too will be committing an offence.

Sports and Pastimes

1. Introduction

Many sports entail some element of danger. This varies from the obvious potential risk to health in boxing to the danger to limbs on the football field or even nowadays on the cricket field. The risk is not confined to participants. Officials, spectators or even passers-by may be injured; such accidents are infrequent but they certainly happen. Sporting activity may also disturb the peace of a locality. Furthermore, tempers are often raised during sport and this may lead individuals to harm others in a manner which would be unthinkable in a different context.

These issues form the bulk of the current discussion. We will not consider the special problems of professional sportsmen or professional clubs. We will emphasise the law as it affects participants and organisers of sporting activity. The latter raises problems such as dangerous equipment or building, inadequate supervision and inadequate fencing of activities. The insurance position both of individuals and of clubs is of great importance. This chapter will not deal with questions of licensing, lotteries and other revenue-raising activities.

2. The Criminal Liability of Participants

A person playing games or being on property where ganes are being played is subject to the ordinary criminal law of the land. There are no special rules if the belongings of other players are stolen from a changing room or if another player is assaulted after an argument in the bar after the game. The same is true if the referee or umpire is deliberately struck. There are, however, special rules applying to injuries caused by one player to another. This is because the normal criminal law makes it a crime to injure someone deliberately or recklessly. In some sports deliberate injury is the objective while in others it is known to be possible. If all injuries inflicted in the course of games were crimes it would of course not be possible for those games to be played; sports like boxing and rugby would take on the illegal status of bear-baiting or cock-fighting.

The Defence of Consent

The law regulates such injuries through the defence of consent. It is possible to consent to being injured if that is the likely or possible outcome of a game. So in a game such as boxing, wrestling or judo, where physical contact is the objective, there is no criminal liability if the fighters stay within the rules. This is the law even in those sad cases where death follows a boxing or other match. The law, however, does not allow a person to consent to the deliberate causing of his own death, a rule which leads to the prohibition of euthanasia. It is different if the death is an accidental, unforeseen result of a deliberate punch or series of punches. Outside boxing, etc a deliberate punch leading to an unexpected death will usually amount to the crime of manslaughter.

The rule that there is no liability for injuries inflicted in boxing and like sports only applies where the game in question is properly organised. There is no special rule for playground fights, for privately organised fights, and probably not for prize-fights, with or without gloves, arranged outside the control of the British Boxing Board of Control or equivalent governing body. In one case decided in 1980 two youths decided to settle their differences in a fight. The injuries sustained were no worse than a bleeding nose and bruising. Although they were acquitted of assault occasioning actual bodily harm, the case was referred to a higher court to enable the law to be clarified. The Court of Appeal said that people may only cause each other deliberate harm in the course of properly conducted games and that most private fights will be illegal even if the participants consent. It makes no difference whether the fight takes place in public or on private property. The effect of this decision is that some relatively normal behaviour in sport is held to be criminal, though the Court said that prosecutions should not be brought in minor cases.

The criminal law has not been used to challenge or outlaw new and potentially dangerous sports such as martial arts and kick-boxing. Some are regulated by official governing bodies and would therefore probably come within the Court's idea of 'properly conducted games.' Others may be run much less formally and there must be a risk that injury to a participant might lead to a prosecution and conviction.

The defence of consent may also be excluded if the injury results from action outside the rules of even a properly organised game. This is true both of games where injury is the objective and those where it is an inherent risk. The law is uncertain, because some activity outside the rules is so likely to cause some injury that it is sensible to say that those taking part accept that risk. It would be strange if the law were that an ordinary soccer foul constituted a crime. The line between legal and illegal behaviour must be socially acceptable. The reason there have been few cases is that traditionally few people injured by opponents have brought a prosecution. In 1978, for example, J.P.R. Williams, the Welsh rugby player, suffered serious facial injuries and the identity of his assailant was known, yet he refused to press charges. That this is a matter of practice, not law, was shown by the important case of *R v Billinghurst*, decided the same year. Again Welsh rugby was involved; here the defendant punched the opposing scrum-half in an off-the-ball incident, fracturing his jaw. The defence argued that the injured person must have consented to being injured in this way as in modern rugby punching is the rule rather than the exception. The judge directed the jury that the test was whether the injury was one 'which could reasonably be expected to happen during a game' and the defendant was convicted and sentenced to nine months' imprisonment suspended for two years.

A recent trend suggests a greater willingness to use the law. In one case David Bishop, a Welsh rugby international, was sentenced to one month's imprisonment after a serious attack on a player well away from the ball. However, on appeal the sentence was suspended. In another case, a Welsh policeman was jailed for six months for biting off part of an opponent's ear during an inter-force rugby match. The law at present is only *used* in the most severe or blatant cases, but any deliberate assault which is clearly abnormal, such as an off-the-ball kick or punch, is a crime; so are things which happen quite frequently, such as punches in a rugby scrum. It is probable, though, that most 'ordinary' soccer fouls will not be crimes unless it can be proved that the motive was to injure; the further away the ball was at the time, the easier it will be to show. Finally, the law holds that a player consents to the risk of injury from a normal rugby tackle, soccer shoulder charge, cricket bouncer and so on.

Children and the Criminal Law

The position of child participants depends on whether they are attackers or attacked. No child under ten can be prosecuted for a crime, and those between ten and fourteen can only be convicted if it can be shown that they knew that what they were doing was clearly wrong. A child victim, on the other hand, is taken to consent to the risk of injury on the same basis as an adult. This is true of junior boxing clubs as well as football and rugby etc; were the law otherwise much physical contact in junior sport would be criminal. As long as the child is aware that some risk is involved parental consent is probably not necessary, though obtaining it is a sensible precaution. Consent applies not just to organised games but also to normal casual play. The principle that consent is only a defence where the game is properly conducted is only applicable to games such as boxing and wrestling where the attack is the essence of the game. In other games it is probable that the law treats casual games, whether involving children or adults, in the same way as more formal games, so that a player is held to consent to the risk of injuries normally resulting. The player who causes such an injury cannot be prosecuted for any offence.

3. The Civil Liability of Participants

The relevant branch of civil law is the law of tort, which is an old word simply meaning 'wrong'. The basis of tort is a claim by one individual against another, unlike crime where the case is brought in the name of the Crown on behalf of the state. The remedy is also different; the claim is that the defendant should compensate the victim (or in some cases stop the offending behaviour) rather than be punished by fine or imprisonment. It is possible for both criminal and civil proceedings to be brought in respect of the same event.

Football Hooliganism

The most obvious examples of hooliganism, whether inside or outside the ground, involve the crimes of assault, theft and criminal damage. If no individual suffers any damage from the behaviour it is still possible that crimes have been committed. These are the public order offences, and include possessing an offensive weapon, threatening behaviour, obstructing a policeman (usually by refusing to obey his orders) and the new offence of disorderly conduct.

Clubs also have the right to refuse entry to a ground for whatever reason, and police have the right to search people before they are allowed to enter. Ejection is also permissible if either the conditions of entry or the criminal law are broken. It follows that clubs may try to prevent the consumption of alcohol on their premises, whether bought there or brought in by spectators. It will be negligence if clubs fail to take reasonable steps to protect members of the public from the consequences of hooliganism: the stewarding and the barricades must be adequate.

There are two possible relevant torts, battery and negligence. Battery is an intentional hostile touching by one individual of another; negligence is the careless infliction of harm. The latter cannot usually lead to criminal proceedings as they normally require that the defendant was aware that his behaviour might cause harm. The defence of consent will always be a defence to the tort of battery if it would have been a defence had criminal charges been brought. Every case where a sportsman commits a crime on the field of play also constitutes the tort of battery and gives rise to a claim for compensation. The same is true of crimes committed in unlawful boxing or wrestling matches or assaults on participants or officials unconnected with the actual play. On the other hand there may be cases where a tort is committed but the behaviour is not also a crime.

The Sportsman's Standard of Care

The other relevant tort is negligence, which usually applies where the harm was not caused intentionally or recklessly but carelessly. Not all carelessly caused harm is a tort; there must be a duty to take care owed by one person to another, a breach of that duty which is defined as the failure to take such care as would have been taken by a hypothetical reasonable person, and finally damage resulting from the breach of duty. There are also certain defences available; no damages are awarded if the injured party accepted the risk of being injured in the way in which he was in fact injured, and damages can be reduced if the injured person was partly to blame for his injuries.

The law is clear that people participating in sport owe a duty of care to anyone who may be affected by their activities, whether other players, spectators or anyone else in the vicinity. The most important question is the test for deciding when that duty has been broken. Here there is a special rule: there is no breach of duty if the player is simply doing his best. If a cricketer hits a six and injures a spectator he is not liable; the same is true if his shot injures a close-in fielder. An example of someone doing his incompetent best is a golfer whose sliced shot injures someone on the next fairway; again, no liability. If a soccer or rugby player slides off the field into a spectator the same rule applies. The principle has even been applied to motor sport. In *Wilks v Cheltenham Home Guard Motor Cycle and Light Car Club* (1971) a motorcycle scrambler left the track and injured a spectator and was found not liable as he was only doing his best; errors of judgement are occasionally bound to happen in racing. For the same reason a rally car which left the road would probably not expose the driver to a negligence claim, though it is absolutely certain that a similar error on an ordinary road would be negligent. There is a possible negligence claim against the organisers if they should not have allowed such an incompetent or inexperienced driver to take part.

The reason for the rule is that a sportsman is often acting in the heat of the moment. If that is not the case then ordinary negligence principles apply. In *Harrison v Vincent* (1981) a racing motor cycle left the course and caused injury. The driver was held negligent as the cause of the accident was careless adjustment of the brakes *before* the race. Again in *Cleghorn v Oldham* (1927) the defendant struck an observer while demonstrating how to play a golf stroke, and was held liable for negligence. Golf is not a game where the heat of the moment principle could ever apply; neither are demonstrations rather than actual play, for example, of hockey or lacrosse techniques. The rule depends on whether it was necessary to take time to reflect on whether it was safe to carry on. If it were, it is still the case that there is normally no liability if a participant has merely done his incompetent best.

The most important case on the issue is *Wooldridge v Sumner* (1963). The accident occurred at a horse show where a rider was galloping his horse along the side of the open-air arena. He took a corner too quickly and the horse veered to the left, injuring a cameraman. The Court of

Appeal held that this was a mere error of judgement which was bound to happen sometimes; only if it was such a serious error of judgement that it would be fair to regard it as having been reckless would the rider be liable for negligence.

It is important that the Court concluded that the rider's standard of care was not broken. This is because it would be unfair to say that the cameraman consented to the risk of being injured as he had no knowledge that horses were liable to behave in such a way. Furthermore, while someone in the front row at Lord's might accept the risk of being injured by a cricket ball, the law holds that young children can never consent to negligence, nor can their parents, so to speak, give consent on their behalf. The rule is different in the case of a child participating in a game which has an unavoidable and obvious risk of injury. The reason why the child in the front row cannot claim damages from the batsman is not that he has consented to run the risk of injury but that the batsman has not been negligent even though he almost certainly appreciates the risk, slight as it is, that his batting may injure someone.

The most difficult question is whether every breach of rules gives rise to a tort claim. The recent case of *Condon v Basi* concerned a claim for damages for a broken leg suffered as a result of a very dangerous but hardly unusual late tackle on the football field. The financial significance of cases like this is shown in that the successful claimant was awarded damages of £4,900. The footballer was held liable because he failed to exercise the degree of care to be expected of a footballer in his position; a player only consents to the risk of injuries which occur as a result of the exercise of proper reasonable care. In this case it was held that there was shown a 'reckless disregard' of safety. It may well now be the law that any breach of the rules leading to injury is a tort; this statement is almost certainly true of rules designed to promote safety and may be true of other rules as well. The law has not yet reached that position, as this case was a flagrant violation, but it is likely to do so soon. On the other hand it is not clear that a Criminal Court would decide that this late tackle was a crime. A different result to *Condon* was reached in a karate case only reported in a Cornish local paper. A 'round-house' kick, described as one of the commonest moves in karate, caused a ruptured spleen, but there was no evidence that the blow was in excess of what could reasonably have been expected to be used, particularly as accidents such as teeth being knocked out and noses broken were said to be not uncommon. Unlike *Condon*, there was no breach of the rules in this case.

A warning of danger may avoid liability for negligence, but only if sufficient to enable the person warned to avoid the danger. In one case a golfer lost his ball in the rough and indicated to his playing partners that they should complete the hole without him. When they had reached the green he found his ball and played another shot. A partner was hit despite the golfer's cry of 'Fore!' The warning was clearly inadequate to enable evasive action to be taken. It is hard to see that a warning by a participant can ever be sufficient, because events will usually be happening very quickly. Warnings are much more likely to be effective in relation to a dangerous state of affairs than a dangerous activity.

4. The Criminal Liability of Organisers

The position of participants and organisers is clearly distinct. If the rally-car is liable to leave the road the question is whether the organisers have a responsibility to prevent injuries occurring. The same is true if golf balls are likely to be hit outside the boundaries of the golf-course. It is easy to think of other examples. The responsibilties of organisers, both in criminal law and in civil law, may arise to both participants, especially children, and to spectators and those off the premises.

Criminal liability will only arise in extreme cases, as the majority of criminal offences require either intention or recklessness, and an organiser is unlikely to have shown more than carelessness. An organiser may be liable in the same way as an ordinary individual if he assaults someone, but that depends on the normal law and not on the fact that he is the organiser.

Manslaughter is the only serious crime which can be committed if the state of mind which lawyers call 'gross negligence' is present. This could apply to organisers, but there appear to be no cases where such a charge has been brought. Imagine, though, a rifle-range; if a participant fired before the all-clear had been given and killed someone it is possible that he could be convicted of manslaughter by gross negligence; if an organiser gave the all-clear at an inopportune moment and the same thing happened he might be liable rather than the marksman. Permitting children to play unsupervised with equipment or machinery known to be extremely danger-ous is another possible example. While not a case involving sport, the events where children were swept off the rocks near Land's End demon-strate the importance of proper supervision. There was no criminal negli-gence in this case, but those teaching climbing, sailing, caving, etc could conceivably find themselves charged with manslaughter if a child or indeed an adult dies as a result of their grossly negligent conduct. There is a major peculiarity in the criminal law relevant here. While it is a crime to cause *death* in a grossly negligent manner, it is not a crime to cause non-fatal injuries through gross negligence, although it is a tort.

There are many other ways in which the criminal law is relevant, especially to sports clubs. Clubs are subject to building and planning regulations in the same way as other owners; licensing and gambling law includes some criminal offences; the Health and Safety at Work Act applies if a club employs staff; food hygiene rules may apply; tax and national insurance may be payable. These issues relate to the organisation and administration of a sports club as opposed to the activities for which the club is in existence. They apply to all clubs, sporting or otherwise, and are not discussed here.

5. The Civil Liability of Organisers

It is here that sports clubs and sporting activity are most likely to fall foul of the law. Damage may be suffered by participants, by spectators, by those on the premises for some other purpose, and by those not on the premises. The question is always whether reasonable care has been taken to ensure that injury does not occur. The law of negligence does not require that organisers *guarantee* that accidents will not happen, merely that reasonable steps are taken to prevent them. Because the concept of reasonableness is flexible and applies to a whole variety of situations it is often impossible to state the law with certainty; all that can be done is to mention factors which courts take into consideration. It is also important that the law holds an employer liable for the torts of his employees committed while they were at work; so if a player is injured as a result of the negligent maintenance of club equipment by a groundsman the club will be liable as well as the individual, and the realities of insurance are such that the club may well be able to pay damages whereas the employee may not. The club will also be liable for torts committed by members acting as such, for example if the equipment were negligently serviced by a club member on a Sunday morning.

(i) Safe Premises
The first duty of a club is to ensure that the club property is reasonably safe, including club buildings where this applies. The duty here is similar to that of an ordinary householder to maintain his property. If someone is injured by a falling tile or a defective floor the occupier of the building is extremely likely to be held liable. This includes making adequate arrangements to have the property repaired. So in *Brown v Lewis* (1896) committee members were held personally liable after an incompetent person had been hired to repair a stand. Similarly in *Francis v Cockrell* (1870) a club was held liable for the collapse of a grandstand. It makes no difference whether or not the injured person has paid to come in; if he has not the case is one of tort and depends on whether the occupier had fulfilled the general duty to take reasonable care, while if he has paid to come in that creates a contract between him and the club. That contract will be held to include a term requiring the occupier to take reasonable steps to ensure that the property is safe for the entrant's purpose, and this imposes the same standard as the tort test. So the same standard is owed by both professional and amateur clubs. In some situations, though, the occupier of the defective building will not be the club but, for example, the local council from whom the club

hired the property. If so the council, not the club, should be sued unless the damage was caused by the activities of a club member.

It may not affect the club's responsibility that the accident happened in a somewhat unexpected way. The principle is that so long as the end result was a reasonably foreseeable consequence of the original act of negligence the club will still be liable. In *Hosie v Arbroath Football Club* (1978) the club knew that a gate was corroded and dangerous. The actual accident happened when spectators charged the gate and it collapsed. While the club was not legally responsible for the activities of spectators, whether on or off club premises, it was foreseeable that this kind of behaviour might occur and that the gate might collapse in consequence. An ordinary amateur club which never sees more than a handful of spectators would probably not be liable if this happened, as it would not be foreseeable. They would be liable, however, if, for instance, a cricketer trying to stop the ball going over the boundary collided with a fence or a pavillion, which then collapsed on him. While that kind of thing only happens very rarely, if ever, it is foreseeable as a possible consequence of negligent maintenance of a sports ground.

(ii) Safe Equipment

The next duty is that owed by organisers to participants. This sub-divides into the duty to ensure that equipment is reasonably safe and the duty to provide adequate supervision. The idea of equipment needs to be interpreted widely. In *Gillmore v LCC* (1938) a gym activity was taking place on a highly polished floor when one of the participants slipped and was injured. The Court held that the floor was unsuitable and that to maximise safety an unpolished floor should have been used. This principle could apply to the use of dangerous cricket nets or a decision to sail in weather unsuitable for the size of yacht, as well as more obvious examples such as defective gymnasium equipment. There is unlikely to be liability, however, if it is apparent to the participants that the organisers or the club have no greater expertise than they do, for the law would then conclude that the former took the risk of injury upon themselves. There is a difference between the provision of defective equipment where the danger is not apparent, such as a yacht whose rudder is broken, and the decision to engage in an activity with some obvious degree of risk. The law recognises that some sports and pastimes carry an obvious and inevitable risk; negligence arises where, through the fault of the organisers, there is a greater risk than is normally present. It would therefore be negligent for an organiser to give the impression of having greater skill and experience than was in fact the case. This principle was illustrated in *Simms v Leigh RFC* (1969) when a Rugby League player suffered a broken leg as a result either of a legal tackle or of colliding with the boundary wall. The evidence was unclear but on either view the claim failed. If the tackle caused the injury no-one was to blame as players consent to the risk of being injured in the normal course of the game; if the collision was the cause the club was not to blame as the wall was the regulation distance from the touch-line, such an accident was not known to have happened before and so the player must be taken to have accepted the risk of this injury which did not occur through negligence.

(iii) Adequate Supervision

The duty to provide adequate equipment and facilities overlaps with the duty to provide proper supervision, for the reasonableness of a decision to proceed will often depend on the experience of the participants and the amount of available supervision. Whether it is negligent to take a party of schoolchildren hill walking in the Lake District when heavy rain is forecast will depend on a number of variables, such as the age of the children, their experience and that of their leader, and how well-equipped they are. This kind of case has reached court so rarely that it is impossible to be dogmatic in advance as to the outcome; two cases are never identical. *Jones v LCC* (1932) shows that it can be reasonable to engage in, or even require participation in, activities with a degree of risk. Unemployed young people 17 years old attended a training centre the activities of which included compulsory physical education. The instructor ordered them to participate in a 'piggy-back fight' in the course of which an injury occurred. It was held not to be negligent to require them to participate in activity with a clear though small risk of injury; the instructor gave evidence that he had seen the game played for twenty years without serious accident. It might be different, if, for example, one pair was very much heavier and stronger than another pair.

The law recognises that supervision cannot prevent all accidents. *Clarke v Bethnal Green BC* (1939) concerned an accident at a swimming pool which occurred when a swimmer let go of the springboard from underneath and catapulted off the person waiting to dive. There were unproved allegations that the attendant was not paying proper attention, but the Court considered that even if this were true the accident could not have been avoided. It was not a risk of which a reasonable swimming-pool attendant should have been specifically aware, and she could not be everywhere at once. Note that the person actually responsible for the accident may have been liable for the damages. It is probable that the responsibility of supervisors is less in individual pastimes, such as riding and beach or pool swimming, than when competitive games are taking place, particularly where adults are taking part.

(iv) Injuries to Spectators

The next question is when organisers are liable for injuries to spectators. We saw that, for example, a cricketer is not liable if his shot hits a spectator; this is true for golfers using proper care but hitting a bad shot, for hockey players and so on. The issue is whether the organisers have a legal duty to protect spectators by fencing or other means. This will depend on numerous factors, such as how likely injury was to occur, how serious any resulting injury was liable to be, and how easy it would be to stop it. A difficulty with explaining the law is that the two most relevant cases might well be decided differently today if the same thing happened. In *Hall v Brooklands Auto Racing Club* (1933) two cars collided and hit the barrier railing, which broke leading to the deaths of spectators. The Court held that reasonable care did not require the strengthening of the barrier as no such accident had occurred in 23 years. Since then speeds have increased enormously, more than 80 people were killed in a similar accident at Le Mans in 1955 and, to give them credit, race organisers now take far greater precautions. In fact the failure to take such precautions as are now normally taken by others would probably be sufficient by itself to show negligence. The problem arises where the circuit is very long, as in the Isle of Man TT or where there is no circuit as in the RAC Rally. Clearly in such cases fencing is impracticable; it is suggested that the duty would be satisfied if the organisers kept spectators away from the points on the course where they knew from experience that accidents were most likely and perhaps also provided barriers in such places if possible. In *Hall* the Court also said that any reasonable spectator accepted the risk of being injured in such a way. This reasoning is dubious as it is wrong to suggest that spectators accept the risk of being injured in a *negligent* manner; furthermore children may be injured and it can never be said that they consent to being injured. In *White v Blackmore* (1972) a spectator at a jalopy race was killed owing to the negligent erection of barrier ropes such that when a car collided with the ropes a main stake was lifted from the ground with great force. The spectator did not consent to the risk because he was unaware that the ropes had been tethered incorrectly; although, as we will see later, his claim failed for a separate reason.

The other case, *Murray v Harringay Arena* (1951), concerned a six-year-old hit in the eye by a puck at an ice-hockey match. He failed in his claim on the ground that there was no duty to guard against a danger which was inherent in the game. This principle seems unnecessarily wide. Pucks are highly dangerous and very likely to be hit above the edge of the rink. It is suggested that there must be a duty to provide fencing high enough to prevent most shots from getting into the crowd. Compared with cricket this would happen far more frequently and be liable to cause far more damage. Of course for most amateur sports clubs the lack of spectators means that injury is less likely and therefore the duty is not as stringent.

For amateurs it is the passer-by who is more at risk: the sliced golf shot hits a pedestrian, the football goes into the road and causes a car-crash and so on. Again, basic principles of negligence law apply and various factors must be weighed. In *Lamond v Glasgow Corporation* (1968) a pedestrian was hit while walking along a lane adjacent to a golf-course. The evidence was that some 6,000 balls per year came over the fence; there was also evidence from golf-course architects that it would be possible to redesign the course at no great cost to reduce that figure. On these facts it was easy to hold the club liable and they would probably have been liable even if redesign had not been possible given the high risk of injury. On the other hand, in *Bolton v Stone* (1951) a passer-by outside a cricket field failed to recover compensation after being hit on the head by a ball. The club had erected a high fence and the evidence was that this was an exceptional hit, balls having cleared the fence only a handful of times in 30 years. The club had taken all reasonable steps to prevent injury. It is clear, though, from *Miller v Jackson* (1972) that if property damage is unavoidable (in this case to a greenhouse with the possibility of damaging houses) the club will have to pay compensation; this would also be true in the unlucky event of injury to people in the house or garden. If it is likely that at some time someone outside the club will suffer damage to his person or his property then it is only in the very exceptional cases like *Bolton v Stone* that the club will not be held negligent. If the ball causes a driver to swerve to take evasive action and an accident results a Court would probably hold that to be a reasonably foreseeable consequence of a failure to contain balls within the ground and so the club or the occupier would be liable. Of course in many situations fencing would either be impracticable or very unsightly (planning permission may be unobtainable) so in theory the club is in an impossible situation, but in practice the risk seems less severe than one might imagine and adequate insurance should be obtainable.

(v) Defences to Negligence

In some situations a club may have been negligent, but yet will not be liable to pay damages because it has a defence. If something is dangerous a warning may avoid liability if people can avoid the danger as a result; such a warning can either be verbal or by a notice. To fix a notice telling people not to use the cricket nets or to skate on a pond will probably be enough, although even then, if the club knows that young children are in the habit of using the facilities, it may have to go further and actually prevent their use. But a warning will be insufficient if the people on one's property have no alternative. To warn about the state of an unlit pathway or drive will not necessarily mean that an injured person cannot sue the occupier. The warning may be inadequate for the same reason that 'Beware, Falling Rocks' is inadequate.

The defence of consent has already been mentioned. It is this which prevents the tort of battery being committed in any contact sport. Children are held to consent by themselves or through their parents, teachers or guardian. But consent is only given to risks normally incident to the game; for this reason there was no defence to the bad foul in *Condon v Basi*. Equally it is virtually impossible to give consent to a negligent act, for consent requires awareness of the risk. Most of the cases where courts have

106

Nuisance

Clubs may also be liable for the tort of nuisance. This is concerned not so much with actual damage to person or property but with interference with one's right to enjoy one's property. In such a case the remedy which is sought will usually be an injunction, which is a Court order that the nuisance should cease.

Typical examples of nuisances are extreme noise or extreme smells. So if a sports club created unusually pungent smells or organised discos which frequently went on late into the night, adjoining property owners could seek an injunction. Whether one would be issued depends on how frequently it happens, how close the neighbouring properties are and how many of them are affected. A Court may grant a compromise order, for example, that no music shall be played later than midnight. Obviously it is cheaper and more neighbourly to attempt to resolve these cases without going to Court; it is only if the situation is very bad that it would be advisable to seek an injunction.

In some cases the actual playing of the game may be the alleged nuisance, and in a serious case the injunction will require the activity to cease altogether. In *Stretch v Romford FC* (1971) the club were required to cease permitting speedway meetings to take place in their stadium. In such a case the nuisance must relate to the actual playing of the game rather than any inconvenience caused by large numbers of spectators with consequent possible parking problems and even vandalism or hooliganism. For these the club is not responsible; were the law otherwise almost every large stadium would have to be shut.

Stretch was a clear case; two other recent cases were less certain. *Miller v Jackson* concerned cricket balls being hit into the gardens of adjoining houses, causing minor damage and preventing the Millers using their garden while cricket was in progress. Despite the undeniable interference, the Court refused an injunction to stop cricket being played. There was no other available pitch in the village and the club was said to be one of the focal points of village life. In other words, the public interest prevailed over the private though the club would have had to pay compensation for any future damage caused by cricket balls. A different result was reached in *Kennaway v Thompson* (1980), where an injunction was sought to restrain power-boat racing on a lake adjoining Mrs Kennaway's house. The judge was able to compromise, so that the club were permitted to continue organising racing, but only on a limited number of weekends during the year and operating under a maximum decibel limit. It will only be in very unusual situations that a sporting activity will cause interference to an extent that a judge will grant an injunction. Residents are expected to put up with the minor inconvenience which is all that will occur in most cases.

said that participants or spectators consented to the risk turn out to be cases where neither the participant nor the organisers were negligent; examples are the cases of *Wooldridge v Sumner* and *Murray v Harringay Arena* discussed earlier. To summarise, the defence of consent, both for children and adults, applies to normal, inevitable risks but not to additional risks which are the result of negligence by either participant or organiser.

The defence of contributory negligence is much commoner than that of consent; this applies where, although negligence caused the injury, the victim was partly to blame through lack of care for his own safety. He still gets some compensation though; the Court decides by what percentage he was to blame and reduces by that percentage the amount of compensation it would have awarded had he been blameless.

One frequently sees on notice-boards, tickets or programmes a statement that the occupier or organiser is not liable for any injury howsoever caused. This is an attempt to avoid having to pay compensation even if an injury is caused through negligence. The Unfair Contract Terms Act 1977 restricts occupiers of *business* premises from relying on such clauses. If personal injury is suffered the attempted exclusion is completely ineffective; the case proceeds as if it were not there, though occupiers have not been stopped from putting them up. If the damage is only to property the defendant may rely on the exclusion if it is reasonable to allow him to do so. Professional sports clubs are business premises and local authorities are specifically included in the definition of business. Amateur clubs are not businesses even if they seek to make money through bar sales, social activities etc. They are therefore permitted to rely on such notices. To do so reasonable steps must be taken to draw people's attention to them. In *White v Blackmore* the claim by the deceased's widow failed because of such a clause inside the programme he was given when he entered the course. The most likely use of such a notice is to try to exclude liability if belongings are stolen from club property. This may happen without any negligence by club members or officials; if so, the notice is unnecessary. But if there is negligence, such as forgetting to lock a door, the notice will mean that the club will not be liable. It must cover what happened; so, if it excludes liability for damage or loss to belongings, it will not work to exclude liability if someone suffers personal injury through negligence.

6. The Need For Insurance

Any sports club which fails to take out adequate insurance is extremely foolish. It is exposing itself to the slight but definite possibility of having to pay large damages. Equally important, it is leaving open the possibility that a member may receive no compensation for a serious injury for which no-one is to blame.

The relevant insurance is of two main kinds, first party and third party. Under the former, payment is received simply upon proof that loss has occurred. The question of who, if anyone, was to blame is irrelevant. The commonest examples of this form of insurance are household contents policies and that part of a comprehensive motoring policy dealing with accidental damage to the vehicle. A club needs to ensure that its own buildings and property are adequately insured. It may also be possible to take out a policy covering the property of private individuals while on club premises and the property of club members while elsewhere but representing the club.

We are accustomed to thinking about first-party insurance as dealing with property, but it is possible to insure people as well. Most sports injuries will not be the result of any tort and there will in all probability be no legal right to damages. Yet each year a number of rugby players are paralysed for life, and serious injuries may occur in most sports. There is no legal obligation on sports clubs to insure their members, and policies can be taken out by individuals, yet very few do so. It is suggested that there is a moral responsibility to protect the interests of members in this way; this is even more true where children are involved who cannot be expected to protect their own interests.

Third-party insurance provides protection not against being injured but against being held liable to pay damages for someone else's injury. Without legal liability no payment is due. There are, as we have seen, many situations in which such a liability can arise, situations where there may have been no more than momentary carelessness. If a club is not insured and is not set up as a limited company any such damages will have to be paid by the club or even in exceptional cases by members of the committee or the individual who was negligent. Most awards of damages are less than £1,000, but in the rare cases of lifetime paralysis or brain damage they can exceed £300,000. The public liability part of a contents policy may or may not cover an individual, but it cannot apply to the liability of his club. The need for and the provision of sports insurance is growing, and clubs should find no difficulty in arranging cover. The potential gap concerns injuries suffered in casual games in the park or on the beach. Here there is no question of club liability; individuals will almost certainly be uninsured in respect of their own injuries and, unless their public liability policy provides cover, in respect of injuries to others. The possibility of an uninsured catastrophic loss is unavoidable.

7. Clubs and Their Members

(i) Discrimination Law

While clubs are in theory private bodies, there are controls on the way membership is regulated. It used to be the law that anyone could be rejected for membership for whatever reason, but the coming of controls on discriminatory behaviour has changed that. Racial discrimination is nearly always unlawful; if a club has less than twenty-five members it may discriminate on racial grounds in respect of who is admitted to membership or the terms of such membership. Also, a club is permitted to discriminate if its purpose is to provide recreational and social benefits to people of a particular nationality, such as London Welsh or Indian Gymkhana, though this exception does not apply to discrimination on ground of colour rather than nationality. The law does not prevent refusal of membership for an adequate reason such as that the club is full or the person has been expelled from a similar club. Clubs with less than twenty-five members are *not* permitted to discriminate in the employment of staff.

The Sex Discrimination Act 1975 also applies to clubs. In this case there is a much wider exception, as non-profit clubs may be restricted to men or women only or have different classes of membershp for women or for men. It is also unlawful to discriminate on grounds of sex or against a married person in the employment of staff. At present this prohibition does not apply if less than five employees are employed, which probably includes most clubs, but legislation going through Parliament in 1986 will remove this 'small firms' exception.

Discrimination law applies to participation in sport as well as club membership. The only permitted instances of race discrimination are where teams are selected on the basis of nationality. Those few clubs permitted to discriminate in team selection are not allowed to discriminate as regards who they will play against or access to club facilities after a game. In other words no club may restrict use of bar facilities to whites only or Indians only. The small clubs exception applies only to membership and not to other facilities which may be offered.

Sex discrimination against participants is a different problem as it is the average lower strength and height of women which puts them at a disadvantage in certain sports, though this difference only appears in the teenage years. The Act provides that sports can be restricted to one sex only where the average women is at a disadvantage compared with the average man. This permits discrimination in most adult sport. *Bennett v Football Association* (1978) concerned a ban on a twelve-year-old girl from playing in league matches. The ban was upheld by the Court on the ground that the Act looks to the average women and not the average girl. It might be possible to argue that such a blanket ban is contrary to European Community Law, but no-one has yet brought an action. There is room for disagreement about whether in a particular case the average woman is at a disadvantage (snooker, darts, bowls?) and it is surprising that more cases have not been brought. Of course the law only *permits* such discrimination; it does not *require* it, so if the sport's governing body agrees, mixed sports are always lawful at whatever age.

(ii) Disciplinary Action

Sometimes a club may wish to descipline or even expel a member. While the Courts are unwilling to intervene very often, there are certain minimum standards with which clubs must comply. Disciplinary action can only be taken if the club is given power to do so by its rules, and then only for reasons specifically stated in the rules. The proper procedures must be followed, so that if, for instance, the rules say that the club secretary must be a member of any disciplinary committee, any decision without his presence will be null and void. The basic rule is simply that the club rules must be strictly complied with. If not, a Court ruling may be sought that the discipline was invalid; this does not prevent the club starting again and carrying out the procedure properly if possible. The club must also comply with the rules of natural justice. There are two. No-one shall be a judge when he has an interest in the matter; for example, if the case arose out of a disagreement between a committee member and an ordinary member, it would be wrong for the committee member to sit on the disciplinary committee. The second rule is that everyone has the right to state his case. This means a right to know in advance of a discipline hearing why the club wants to impose discipline and a chance to speak in one's own defence.

In the sporting context discipline is more likely to be imposed by the sport's governing body; suspensions are the most common cases. Again the Courts are reluctant to intervene. The same principles apply however: the disciplinary body must comply both with its own rules and with the rules of natural justice. As long as the procedure is basically fair there is no right to be represented by a lawyer, although the particular procedure may allow it. There is no right actually to appear before a tribunal, merely an opportunity to put one's defence either orally or in writing. The Courts consider such bodies to be expert and therefore do not encourage what are in effect appeals to the Courts unless there has been basic unfairness in the procedure.

Using the Countryside

Every inch of the countryside is owned by someone. It is trespass to go onto someone's land without authority – which means either their permission or some legal right. But the public are able to use large parts of the countryside, including some commons, and all public rights of way and country parks.

1. Rights of Way

The commonest way to get out and enjoy the countryside is by using part of the 120,000 miles of public rights of way. A public right of way is a route which any member of the public can use, for a journey, or simply for recreation.

There are three categories of public right of way:

Footpaths which can be used on foot, with a dog or with other things such as prams which a pedestrian may have.

Bridleways which can be similarly used by pedestrians and also by persons with horses, animals driven in a pack and by pedal cyclists.

Byways open to all traffic which can be used by all these, and vehicles.

Maps also sometimes refer to **RUPPs**: roads used as a public path. All RUPPs are gradually being converted into one of the other classes of right of way – usually a bridleway or byway. Until they are converted the public can certainly walk, ride a horse or bicycle along them and may be able to drive a motor vehicle depending on the particular path. The county council should be able to advise on each path.

Long distance routes, heritage walks, recreation paths and coastal paths have no special legal status; they are simply a series of paths which have been joined together into a longer route. However, canal-side towpaths are special. In law they are provided by canal owners for use by people towing boats on the canal. In some places the canal owner has also given the public a right to use the towpath for walking or riding. When the public are allowed to use a towpath users must give way to people using the canal. A sign to use the towpath will indicate the conditions on which the public may use it. 'Green lanes' have no legal status. There may be no public right to use them at all, although many are byways.

The public only have the right to pass and repass along a right of way. There is not right to wander off the path onto adjoining land – unless the path is so muddy or obstructed it cannot be used, in which case a user can go onto nearby land just as far as is needed to get round the obstruction. The public can stop for a rest, and generally picnicking is accepted, but camping on the path or its verge is not lawful. The person becomes a trespasser and may be guilty of obstruction.

(i) How to Find Rights of Way

The easiest way to find out where there are rights of way is by looking at an Ordnance Survey Map – notably the 1:25,000 Pathfinder Series – but the Ordnance Survey do not guarantee that any routes shown on the map are usually public rights of way. Most of the time these maps are accurate enough, but if there is any doubt the county council or (borough) should be consulted, for they are required to maintain an up-to-date 'Definitive Map' – which is just what it says it is. In law, that is the correct statement of public rights of way. If a way is on the map that right along that route exists. The map is conclusive evidence that the rights shown do exist, but it does not prove that rights not on the map do not exist – only that nobody has put them on the map yet, so if people are sure of their facts, they may use a public right of way which is not on the Map. Details of the procedure for getting the Definitive Map altered may be obtained from county councils. The process of updating maps is time consuming so most are out of date with a backlog of claims. Nonetheless, a claim should be made as soon as an error is discovered, if only to reserve a place in the queue!

The Definitive Map not only contains the route of a right of way, it also has notes concerning some rights of way, for example, details of their width. Otherwise it is difficult to find out how wide a right of way should be, as there is no legally prescribed width. In the absence of any other evidence, if a way is enclosed on both sides it is reasonable to assume the entire space between each hedge or fence is part of the right of way. Although the width of the right of way itself is not fixed by law, any gates on a bridleway must be at least 1.5 metres (5ft) wide.

The county council must ensure there is a sign wherever a footpath, bridleway or byway leaves a metalled road, giving details of the class of route, its destination and its distance. Any council or the landowner may waymark routes, by putting small markers along the route, to ensure users can find the way. The landowner's consent is needed to install them. Detailed advice, including the standard colour codes for waymarking arrows and the legal requirements can be obtained from the Countryside Commission. Any member of the public may take the county council to Court to enforce their obligations.

(ii) Maintenance

For most public rights of way, if the landowner declines to take action, the highway authority (the county council, metropolitan district council or London borough council) has an obligation to keep them maintained, and district and parish councils have a range of powers to assist. This means keeping the surface of the path in good order, as long as the path exists, but where a path ceases to exist, such as a cliff path collapsing into the sea, the council is not obliged to restore it. The standard of maintenance varies according the use of the path. As a judge said in one case, you cannot expect the same standard for a family walking to church on Sunday and someone out for a rural ramble. Department of Environment guidelines state that:

> 'where paths are used mainly for pleasure by ramblers, it will no doubt generally be sufficient that they should be free from obstructions or impassable water or mud . . . The main requirement is clearly that they should serve their purpose, whether business or pleasure, and not that they should conform to some arbitrary standard of construction.'

(iii) Obstructions on the Way

The commonest complaint when using a right of way is to find it obstructed by an overgrown hedge, wired-up gates or ploughing. It is an offence for anyone wilfully to obstruct a right of way, including the landowner, even if the obstruction does not totally block the way, as long as part of the path is interfered with. If a right of way is obstructed, details should be given to the county council.

If the obstruction has a natural cause, such as a rock fall, the county council itself must clear the path as quickly as possible. Otherwise the landowner is legally responsible for maintaining things like gates and fences, keeping hedges trimmed and so on. If he declines to take action, the county council may, on due notice, remove the obstruction and recover their costs from the person responsible for the obstruction. In addition anyone can prosecute a person for obstruction or can take the county council to Court for an order requiring them to carry out their duty to keep the way free from obstructions. A court cannot compel an offender to remove an obstruction, but it may be able to fine the person a continuing sum per day until the obstruction is removed. A person using a path can only remove just so much of the obstruction as is necessary to allow him to continue his journey, for example, by untying a gate. If he can get round without removing the obstruction, he cannot interfere with the obstruction. Deliberate parties of people going out to remove obstructions are unlawful, unless they are doing so with the consent of the highway authority or landowner, and they could be sued for trespass or prosecuted for criminal damage.

Gates are allowed on all rights of way, but stiles are only permitted on

114

footpaths. The landowner must maintain them in a safe condition. If he fails to do so the county council can carry out the repairs and send the bill or obtain a Court order requiring him to carry out repairs. If a landowner voluntarily maintains stiles or gates on public rights of way on his land, he can claim 25% of the cost from the county. The consent of the county council is needed to erect a new stile or gate across a right of way.

The biggest cause of obstructions is ploughing. The occupier of farm land is entitled to plough up a footpath or bridleway which crosses a field, but not one which runs round the edge of a field, but he must restore the surface so as to make it reasonably convenient for the public to use the path within two weeks from the time when he began to plough. If he is prevented from doing so by exceptional weather conditions, he must make the path usable as soon as practicable. Not to do so is an offence for which continuing fines may be imposed for every day the obstruction continues after conviction. Again the county council must enforce this law, but district and parish councils also have powers to do so. A Code of Practice giving guidance to farmers has just been published by the Countryside Commission.

(iv) Interference and Intimidation
Any unreasonable interference with the use of rights of way may lead to prosecution or a civil action, by the landowner or a user. If anyone threatens, intimidates or harasses someone using a right of way, for example by ordering the user to leave or by keeping a fierce dog beside the path, this is an offence which should be reported to the county council. An individual may also be entitled to bring a private prosecution. Misleading signs which are likely to deter people from using a public right of way are also unlawful; again the county council should be informed.

(v) Injury
A landowner, across whose land a right of way runs is not liable for injury to people using the right of way unless he has done something to cause the injury. If he has merely failed to maintain his land he may not be liable. A user of a right of way can sue his fellow users, if they negligently cause him injury. If a person is injured because of the state of the surface of the way, the county council may be liable if it has failed to take reasonable care to ensure the highway is safe. This does not mean the path must be absolutely safe, but that the council must have a system of inspecting paths regularly (how often a path should be inspected depends on the money the county has available, and the importance of the path). But it is rare for people to succeed in getting compensation for injuries on footpaths in the country-side, because the courts do not expect councils to carry out frequent inspections.

(vi) Acquiring Public Rights of Way
Publics rights of way can arise in a number of ways. In most cases a right of

way is dedicated by the owner of the land it crosses. Sometimes the landowner may sign a statutory declaration saying the way has been created or otherwise expressly declare he is creating a path, but more usually he simply lets use begin. After twenty years of use by the public as of right, the path becomes a public right of way and cannot be lost by disuse. Extra rights on public paths can also be acquired in the same way, so if a footpath is used by horses without challenge for twenty years the footpath will become a bridleway. To establish a public right of way, there must be evidence that the way had been used by the public, not just a small group – such as the landowners' staff or friends – and the use must be open, that is, people must have used it believing they had a right to the land without challenge. If the public are using a path which a landowner does not want to become a public right of way and 20 years' use has not yet passed the landowner must take steps to show he is not intending to create a public right of way and does not want the public to use the land. The safest way to do that is to deposit a formal notice with the local authority stating he is not dedicating a highway, together with a 6″ to the mile map showing the routes accepted as public rights of way, declaring that no others are intended. Such a statement lasts for five years.

Alternatively, he can take steps to interrupt use. Whether any steps are sufficient to stop a right of way being created is a difficult question and depends on its own facts. Putting up a notice prohibiting the public is probably not enough, unless the public obey it and stop using the way. Traditionally landowners have closed paths for one day a year, but that is a far from certain way of preventing dedication – indeed the Courts have said it may not be effective in some cases, nevertheless people still continue to do it. Even putting up a 1.5 metres (5 ft) fence across the way may not be enough – it will depend on the reason for the fence.

(vii) Closing or Diverting Rights of Way
Rights of way cannot cease to exist through disuse – once a highway always a highway. They can only be closed or diverted if the way is not needed or there is a more convenient route. In most cases closure or diversion orders are made by the county or district council. Notices must be placed in the local press, and on the paths affected, with a plan showing the effect of the order. These signs have to be legible but are not always large. The notice specifies the closing date for objections, which must be at least 28 days away. If there are not objections the county or district council which made the order may confirm the order, but if there are objections the order together with the objections are sent to the Secretary of State for the Environment, who may hold a public inquiry before reaching a decision. As an alternative a right of way may be closed by a Magistrates' Court, on application from a county council.

There are special rules for closing rights of way when someone is going to build on the land. If there are any objections a public inquiry is held. There are also special powers to close rights of way temporarily or permanently for defence purposes.

(vii) Temporary Closure

Right of way and other public land my be closed during outbreaks of diseases such as foot and mouth. In addition there are a number of powers in Local Acts of Parliament to close land in certain circumstances. In each case, a sign will be put up. Local authorities will have details of what is happening. It is a criminal offence to disobey these restrictions. Traffic Regulation Orders, issued by a county council, can restrict or prohibit all, or some use of a public right of way – either on a temporary or permanent basis. Notices of orders must be published in a local newspaper, and a sign must be maintained on the site as long the Order applies. It is an offence to disobey an order. They are commonly used to prohibit all traffic for roadworks, or major sport events, or to control one type of user such as motorcyclists.

2. Other Places to Use in the Countryside

(i) Commons

There is a widespread misunderstanding about what a common is. In law, a common is any piece of land registered under the Commons Registration Act 1965, as being land over which commoners have certain agricultural rights such as grazing cattle or taking wood. In this legal sense, large tracts of uplands, urban commons, and many village greens, heaths and recreation areas may be commons. The common is owned by someone – usually the Lord of the Manor, a company or a local authority. As such it is private land, like any other; the difference is that some people called 'commoners' have extra rights over the land. To be a commoner, the person's rights must be registered with the county council prior to 1970. The extent of those rights depends on local history.

There is no automatic right of the public to use commons for recreation, although that right does exist on many commons, particularly those in built-up areas. Where the public do have a right to use some commons for recreation, there are normally bye-laws controlling that use. Although the laws giving the public the right to use commons for recreation are all over 60 years old, there are still many uncertainties in the law; for example, lawyers are still disputing whether horses may be ridden on commons, except on defined bridleways. The county council maintains a register of commons listing existing commoners rights and the name of the owner and will also know the extent of any general public rights to use the common for recreation. Landowners cannot build on commons, without consent from the Department of the Environment, even for recreation. An application to build has to be advertised in a local newspaper and at least 28 days allowed for comments. The prime factor is whether the building will be of benefit to the whole neighbourhood, not just a limited number of people – so public sports fields and pavilions will generally be allowed, private houses will not.

(ii) Parks, Country Parks and Open Spaces

Many areas of unbuilt land are owned by local authorities for the public use, and are often said to 'publicly owned land', or 'public open space'. Nonetheless this does not give the public unlimited right to use the land. If the land was purchased as a park or open space any member of the public may use it for recreation, subject to any bye-laws or regulations restricting activities. These will be displayed at the entrance to the land. It is an offence to disobey bye-laws. Charges can be made for facilities such as boating, bowls, or picnicking. A country park is simply a park in the countryside, and is subject to the same sorts of legal controls as other parks.

(iii) National Parks

The ten National Parks cover 13,600 square kilometres of land, mainly in the mountains and moorlands. There are special laws which protect the landscape, but there is no general right of public access to land in National Parks. Exactly the same rules about access apply to National Parks as anywhere else.

(iv) Nature Reserves

Nature reserves are designed to assist in conservation. Some are therefore not open to the public, although others allow the public to visit the reserve, on conditions. The first step is to find out who owns the Nature Reserve, and approach the owner for permission to use it. The owner will give details of the special rules which apply to the site.

(v) Permitted Access

In addition to these general legal rights to use the countryside, there are many places the public can use, with the consent of the owner. If an owner is allowing the general public to use his land, the public must obey the conditions he imposes. Some landowners do this by entering an access agreement with the council. This guarantees the public use of the land for a longish period, but in return the landowner can obtain bye-laws to help regulate what people do on his land. Breach of a bye-law is an offence.

3. What Can Be Done in the Countryside

(i) Vehicles

It is an offence to drive a vehicle on a footpath and driving on a bridleway is

> **What are bye-laws?**
> These are made by local authorities and other public bodies, confirmed by the Home Office. It is an offence to break them, for which a person can be prosecuted and fined – although the fines are generally very low. If a person persistently disobeys a bye-law a High Court injunction could be obtained, breach of which could result in imprisonment, so indirectly bye-laws do have some teeth. An authority can change bye-laws with the consent of the Secretary of State.

trespass, unless the landowner has given consent. Vehicles, including motorcycles and cars, can use any byways, although great care must be taken as other users may not be expecting vehicles.

A motor vehicle cannot be driven onto a field, common or open land, even to park, whether or not the public is allowed to use the land for walking, unless the landowner has given permission. It is a criminal offence to do so. It is sometimes said the public can park anywhere within 14 metres of a road. This is not true; although it is not a criminal offence, it is still trespass. However, people can park on verges, providing they do not obstruct gates or other road users.

People often think that motorcycles have no place in the countryside, but many grassed rights of way are, in fact, ancient roads, which cars and motorcycles are permitted to use. In Wiltshire, for example, the old main road from London is now a muddy right of way in places because, when the road was surfaced at the turn of the century, a new route was chosen. People out for a quiet day in country often complain about the presence of motorcyclists – but they may have as much right as anyone else to be there. In extreme cases a Traffic Regulation Order can be used to ban motor vehicles from a particular right of way or the right of vehicular use can be extinguished.

(ii) Animals

It is an offence to keep any dangerous animal in such a way as to endanger members of the public. But even normally harmless animals can sometimes cause injury or damage. An owner is responsible for what his dogs or livestock do, including any injury or damage caused by the animal, if the owner has been negligent in some way. For example, if a cow strays onto the road and damages a car, the owner will be liable if the cow escaped because he had not maintained fences, but he will not liable if it escaped because a rambler left a gate open. Anyone taking an animal onto a right of way or other public place must similarly take reasonable care, and should be suitably insured.

Bulls are a special case. It is an offence to keep a bull in a field or enclosure crossed by a public right of way unless (a) the bull is under eleven months old or (b) is not from the following breeds: Ayrshire, British

Friesian, British Holstein, Dairy Shorthorn, Guernsey, Jersey and Kerry and is accompanied by cows or heifers. Even if a bull falls within one of these two categories, its owner can be liable for any injury it causes, if the owner knew it to be dangerous.

Dogs are also subject to special controls. First, local authorities can designate particular roads as requiring any dogs to be kept of a lead and may have bye-laws prohibiting dogs from fouling footpaths. Secondly, dogs in any public place must have a collar, stating the owner's name and address. Thirdly, if a dog is a danger to people or other animals and not kept under proper control, the police or local authority can take action, or an individual can bring a private prosecution. One complaint will seldom be sufficient to prove the dog is dangerous, hence the comment that dogs are allowed two bites. Certainly the police are reluctant to take action on only one incident; nonetheless serious incidents should be reported in case of further incidents. A Court can require the owner to keep the dog under control, or order the dog to be destroyed. It is an offence for a dog to 'worry' livestock on agricultural land if it could reasonably be expected to cause injury or suffering to the livestock. If the dog actually injures cattle or poultry, or chases sheep, action can be taken to Courts, as if it were a dangerous dog. A farmer can only shoot a trespassing dog where there no other way to prevent serious injury to a person or animal.

(iii) Horses
No licence is needed to keep or ride a horse. Many of the laws concerning traffic do not apply to horses, but there are additional restrictions on horses. The highway code should be obeyed. Councils may prohibit horses using particular grass verges along the roadside. It would be an assault to ride a horse so as to injure someone, and indeed, to ride a horse furiously, so as to obstruct, annoy or endanger the public, is an offence. Riding schools require licensing from the local authority, and must comply with stringent regulations concerning insurance.

(iv) Metal Detecting
The publics may carry and use metal detector in the countryside, but must not disturb the ground surface to remove anything discovered. To do so is trespass, and may also be a criminal offence.

(v) Litter
It is offence to drop any litter in a public place, including streets, parks and on rights of way. Local bye-laws may also make it an offence to drop litter in other places. It is also an offence to dump larger items, such as furniture or garden refuse anywhere, except in an authorised dump.

(vi) Boating
The public can boat and sail on the sea, and on all tidal rivers, up to the top

120

point at which it is tidal. Local bye-laws can regulate boating close to the shore. This is commonly done at popular seaside resorts. Such rules should be displayed somewhere along the shore line, but the sign may not be easily visible. To be sure, check with the local authority.

On all other waterways – other parts of rivers, canals, lakes – people may only boat if there is a public right of navigation (like a right of way, but on the water), or the owner of the land adjoining the river gives consent. Launching, mooring and landing boats also requires the consent of the owner of the bank, unless the public have acquired rights to do so.

When the waterway is owned by a public body the terms on which the public may use the waterway will be displayed at the site as regulations or bye-laws. If you are in doubt, the local authority should know where to find them. Canals are subject to regulations laid down by the British Waterways Board, which require a licence obtainable from the Board for sailing pleasure boats on canals.

Local navigation rules apply in many places in addition to the normal rules for sailing. Just as with driving a car, a person will be liable for any damage he causes negligently whilst sailing. Insurance is not compulsory, but is therefore highly advisable.

4. At The Seaside

The area between high and low water marks, the foreshore, is owned by the Crown, but is usually administered by a local council. The foreshore can be used by anyone for recreation, although bye-laws may regulate what can be done on the foreshore, and the water out to 1,000 metres from low water; for example, swimming may be restricted for safety or conservation. The public may be excluded from foreshores used by bodies such as the Ministry of Defence, but it is safe to presume the foreshore is public, unless a sign says otherwise. A local authority will confirm whether the sign is correct.

The land above high water mark is often owned by the local authority at popular seaside resorts, but some beaches are owned by other people, who may, or may not choose to allow the public to use their beach, just as they can choose to let the public use any other land they own. They cannot prevent the public from using the foreshore, between their land and the sea, but can prevent the public crossing their private land to get to the foreshore or sea, unless there is a public right of way.

Everything on a beach is owned by the landowner. In some case there are customary rights for local residents to remove sand, gravel, or their substances from the beach, but in most places removing shells or pebbles is unlawful, and could be theft as well as trespass – although the landowner would be hard put to show he had suffered damage as a result. Abandoned or unidentifiable objects found loose on the beach may be taken, although they should be reported to the police. When objects apparently from a wreck are found, they must be handed to the local Receiver of Wrecks. Unclaimed material from wrecks belongs to the Crown.

5. Protecting the Countryside

Many laws seek to protect the countryside. Users of the countryside are affected by some, notably the laws protecting wild birds, animals and plants. When animals, birds or plants are protected it is an offence to destroy or interfere with them, even if the person does not realise they are protected, although, if a motorist accidentally kills a protected bird or animal, it is not an offence – but it is an offence to take the bird or animal home if it is game, unless the driver has a game licence.

(i) Birds

All wild birds, except game birds and those regarded by law as pests, are protected. It is criminal offence to kill or injure them, or interfere with their nest or eggs. But damaging any bird, nest or egg from the list of specially protected birds is a particularly serious offence.

Apart from the black-headed gull and common gull (and the lapwing if the eggs are taken between 1 January and 15 April), wild birds' eggs cannot be sold without the consent of the Department of the Environment (Countryside and Recreation Division), the Nature Conservancy Council or the Ministry of Agriculture.

There are few exceptions to these controls though even a protected bird can be destroyed on humane grounds. Landowners can kill birds, except protected birds, if they are interfering with crops. Species regarded as pests may be killed and their nests and eggs destroyed, but only by the land-owner or someone acting for him. If the birds are on publicly owned land someone authorised by a local council, a water board or the Nature Conservancy Council can act.

Birds considered as pests are: collared dove; crow; domestic pigeon now wild; gulls, lesser and greater; black-backed, herring; house sparrow; jackdaw; jay; magpie; rook; starling; wood pigeon.

(ii) Animals

Unlike birds, many animals receive no protection. The only protected animals are otters, bats, sand lizards, great crested or warty newts, smooth snakes, red squirrels, natterjack toad, badgers and seals. It is an offence to interfere with these animals, or their nests or shelters except to prevent serious damage to property or with the permission of the Ministry of Agriculture or Nature Conservancy Council. Licences can be obtained to

122

Specially protected birds
Avocet
Bee-eater
Bewick's swan
Bittern and little Bittern
Black redstart
Black-tailed godwit
Black-winged stilt
Bluethroat
Brambling
Bunting, cirl, Lapland and snow
Chough
Common quail
Corncrake
Crossbill
Diver
Dotterel
Eagle, white and golden
Fieldfare
Firecrest
Garganey
Golden oriole
Goshawk
Grebe, black-necked and
Slavonian
Greenshank
Gull, little and Mediterranean
Gyr falcon
Harrier
Hobby
Honey buzzard
Hoopoe
Kingfisher
Leach's petrel
Long-tailed duck
Merlin
Osprey
Owl, barn and snowy
Peregrine
Plover, Kentish and little-ringed
Purple heron
Red kite
Red-backed shrike
Red-necked phalarope
Redwing
Ruff
Sandpiper, green, purple and wood
Scarlet rosefinch
Scaup
Scoter, common and velvet
Serin
Shorelark
Short-toed treecreeper
Spoonbill
Spotted crake
Stone curlew
Temminck's stint
Tern, black, little and roseate
Tit, bearded and crested
Warbler, Cetti's, Dartford,
    marsh and Savi's
Whimbrel
Whooper swan
Woodlark

From 21 February to 31 August at sea or on the seashore, and from 1 February to 31 August elsewhere Goldeneye ducks, Pintail ducks, Grey-lag Goose (in some places) are also protected.

control badgers or seals. In all cases involving rare species, advice should be sought from the local authority before taking action.

It is an offence to possess or to sell any of the protected animals or an adder, common frog, viviparous lizard, palmate newt, smooth newt, slow worm, grass snake, common toad. Animals which are considered pests, such as foxes, rats and coypu may be killed.

It is an offence to release into the wild any animal which is not normally resident or visitor here, because they can damage the ecological balance. It is also an offence to release animals which exist in the wild, but are unwelcome: coypu, prairie dog, fat dormouse, mongolian gerbil, mink, black rat, grey squirrel and some reptiles. These offences both are subject to unlimited fines.

No animals, not even pests, can be killed by inhumane means such as snares, explosives, or decoys, and for some species the restrictions on methods of killing are even tighter, such as badgers, bats, dormice, hedgehogs, shrews, red squirrels and seals. Nor can automatic weapons, bows, explosives or light be used to help kill or catch wild mammals, except under licence. Only pests can be killed by poisoning.

(iii) Insects

The protecting of endangered species extends as far as insects. It is an offence to kill, injure, catch or possess any protected insect, or disturb its nest or home, except to protect property. But the spider in the bath can still be washed away, providing he does not feature on the list.

(iv) Trees

Tree Preservation Orders impose severe penalties on anyone who cuts down, uproots or destroys any tree subject to such an order, or damages, tops or lops it in such a way that he is likely to destroy it, even if the person does not know of the TPO. A Crown Court can impose unlimited fines. Once the order is made, it is only lawful to interfere with the tree with the consent of the district council, or if the tree is dead, diseased or dangerous. The order can cover a single tree, an entire wood, or all the larger trees in an area. If an order is made in respect of a tree on someone's land he may appeal against the order within 28 days of its being made. Anyone can ask a district council to make a tree preservation order. Department of the Environment guidelines advise authorities to agree to them where the tree is enjoyed by the public and there is a risk of damage to it. The district council keeps a list of trees which are covered by order; it is open to the public. If it is feared a landowner may fell a tree before an order is imposed, it is possible to get the council to take emergency action in secret. Bushes, hedgerows and young trees fall outside this protection, and have no special status, unless the belong to a rare species or form part of a Site of Special Scientific Interest (SSSI).

Quite apart from TPOs, if a landowner wishes to fell trees on his land, even if it is a solitary tree, he may need a licence from the Forestry Commission. The Commission should be consulted, as it is an offence to fell a tree without a licence where one is needed. There may also be additional local restrictions, for example in conservation areas. Details of these may be obtained from the local authority.

(v) Flowers and Plants

The casual user of the countryside has seldom been known to try to take an entire tree home in his pockets, but may be tempted to pick an attractive flower, or dig up a root which would look just right in the garden.

Plants belong to the landowner, who can sue others for removing a plant, although he would have show actual damage. It is also a criminal offence to pick or uproot wild plants (except mushrooms and fungi) without the landowner's consent. If the plants are cultivated, or wild plants are picked for sale, it may also be theft.

Certain plants are protected even from action by their owner, because of their rarity. The only people who can authorise their picking or uprooting are the Nature Conservancy Council. It is not an offence to destroy even the rarest of plants if it is an incidental effect of proper farming or forestry, such as the destruction of ancient meadows by modern chemicals. In such cases the only protection is to designate the land a Site of Special Scientific Interest, when the landowner receives compensation in exchange for restrictions on what he may do on the land.

In a nature reserve, it is an offence to pick or uproot any plant, even a common one, with the same penalty as if it were a protected plant. Local authorities and the Nature Conservancy Council can designate nature reserves, but these will normally be clearly signposted. If they are not, it may be possible to avoid conviction.

(vi) Hunting

The laws concerning hunting are complex. A licence may be needed, but additionally there are restrictions on when hunting can occur and how it may be carried out.

A game licence is needed before it is lawful to hunt for rabbits and 'game birds', ie pheasant, partridge, grouse, snipe, woodcock and capercaillie, but a licence is not required to hunt foxes. A licence is needed to hunt deer, unless the hunting is with hounds, or on enclosed land. No licence is needed for hare coursing – that is, using greyhounds to pursue hares. A licence is also needed to sell game. Game licences can be obtained from Post Offices, or local councils. There are three types:

(a) Red licence – lasts for a year from 31 July;
(b) Green licence – from 1 August to 31 October;
(c) Blue licence – from 1 November to 31 July.

Special fourteen day licences can also be obtained.

Anyone found on land with a gun or dog, if he is thought to be hunting, can be asked to produce a game licence by the owner of occupier of the land, a gamekeeper, the police, an official from the local authority or even by anyone who has a game licence. If the person does not have a licence with him he must give his name and address and details of where the licence was obtained, so that this can be checked.

When hunting is unlawful – close seasons
Close season for birds
1 Feb to 11 Aug
Common snipe

1 Feb to 31 Aug
Common redshank
Coot
Curlew (not stone curlew)
Godwit, bartailed
Golden Plover
Moorhen
Widgeon

1 Feb to 31 Aug (inland)
(starts 21 Feb at sea or foreshore)
Common pochard
Gadwall
Goldeneye
Goose, Canada, greylag, pink-footed, white-fronted
Mallard
Pintail
Scaup
Shoveler
Teal
Tufted duck

1 Feb to 30 Sept
Capercaillie
Woodcock

Close season for hares and rabbits
Hares cannot be sold between 1 March and 31 July.
Anyone who owns or rents enclosed arable land can kill rabbits or hares at any time of year, except hares cannot be killed on Christmas Day or Sundays. But someone who owns or rents land which is NOT enclosed cannot kill rabbits or hares between 1 April and 31 August, and in addition cannot shoot them between 1 September and 10 December.

Close season for deer
Red and Sika deer stags and fallow deer bucks – 1 May to 31 July.
Red and Sika deer hinds and Roe deer does 1 March to 31 October.
Roe deer bucks 1 November to 31 March.

In addition to a licence, the consent of a landowner is always needed to hunt on his land, or it will amount to trespass and possibly also theft. If a hunt enters land without permission, the occupier can sue the Master of the Hunt and any huntsmen he can identify for trespass, and for any injury or damage caused by the hunt. Anyone can prosecute a huntsman who causes an animal unnecessary suffering. It is also possible to obtain an injunction, preventing the hunt from entering land in the future, although many Courts seem reluctant to grant such injunctions.

The law imposes limits as to when hunting for some creatures can take place, even if the animal is bred for hunting. No bird or animal can be hunted between one hour after sunset and one hour before dawn, except on a person's own land. In addition there are close seasons for many birds and animals during which time they must not be hunted at all. Some are related to breeding seasons, but others have no apparent rationale – such as the law that hares must not be killed on Sundays or Christmas Day.

During close seasons it is an offence to kill the species, except to protect crops, or with the consent of the Ministry of Agriculture.

(vii) Poaching

Poaching is hunting on someone's land without their permission or in breach of the law, at the wrong time or without a licence. Whilst people are no longer transported for poaching, it remains a criminal offence even if the person catches nothing. A person may be convicted even if he has not fired a shot, but appears to be intending to poach. If a person fires at a bird from land he is authorised to be on, it is nonetheless poaching to move onto neighbouring land without authority to collect the kill. It is a more serious offence to poach at night. Substantial fines are possible, and the poaching equipment may be confiscated by the Court.

(viii) Fishing

There are no general protections for fish, unlike birds. Fishing in the sea and tidal water is lawful at all times, unless local bye-laws prohibit it. Tidal waters extend up stream on rivers to the point where fresh water begins, or the tidal effect is no longer noticeable – which can be tens of miles.

The rights to fish in a river or lake belong to the person who owns the banks, unless he has sold it to someone else. The owner of the bank of a river generally owns the river bed, and the fishing rights to the mid point in the river. To fish in river, pond, lake or canal without permission from the owner of the fishing rights is trespass and theft, so a person risks prosecution and the confiscation of tackle and catch. However, landowners frequently lease out fishing rights to individuals or clubs. In that case the people who have rented the fishing rights have exclusive use of them and can take action against trespassers. This means the easiest way to fish lawfully is to join an angling club or obtain a licence from a landowner to fish a particular stretch of water.

As well as getting permission from the landowner, an angler may also need a licence from the fisheries officers of the water authority, or from Post Offices and fishing tackle shops in areas where fishing is popular. The fee varies from area to area. Although the law does not require licences everywhere a licence is needed in most parts of the country. The terms of licences vary and must be read carefully, but most license one person to use one rod, and cover a particular type of fishing, although if someone owns fishing rights along a stretch, a licence can be obtained from him which covers anyone using the stretch with his consent in writing. Fishing without a licence where one is required is an offence, but if a fish which falls outside the licence is caught accidentally, that is not an offence providing the fish is returned to the water immediately.

Close season for fish
Salmon 1 Nov to 31 Jan.
Trout 1 Oct to last day of Feb.
Coarse fish 15 March to 15 June.
These can all be varied by local bye-laws.
Bye-laws also regulate rainbow trout fishing in some places. Before fishing, variations should be checked locally. The dates are different for Scotland.

As with other hunting, there is a close season for some species, and turbot, dolphins and porpoises cannot be caught or killed without a special licence.

The use of explosives, poisons and electrical devices, as well as being dangerous, is illegal inland or at sea, as is ensnaring fish by lights, fish roe bait, firearms, gaff, spear, wire or snares.